GERMANY

Popular History of Jewish Civilization

General Editor: Raphael Posner

GERMANY

Compiled by Stuart Cohen

LEON AMIEL PUBLISHER
New York–Paris

Published in the Western Hemisphere by
LEON AMIEL PUBLISHER
New York – Paris

ISBN 8148-0607-4

Printed in Israel

CONTENTS

INTRODUCTION

Centuries before the unification of the separate states into one Germany, the Jews saw that region as one unit, which they called *Ashkenaz,* and which more or less coincides with the borders of Germany. Because of its geographical position the Jewish community of Germany exercised a profound influence on the whole of European Jewry, eastern as well as western. Communities far beyond its borders prayed from its prayer books, adopted its customs, and were molded by the impact of its religious and cultural movements. Indeed the very term Ashkenazi became the accepted description for European Jewry as a whole, just as the term Sephardi, from the Hebrew word for Spain, has come to embrace the many strands of Oriental Jewry. Sad it is to reflect that both these seminal communities were uprooted in their fullest efflorescence, the latter by the fury of the Inquisition, the former by the terror of the Holocaust.

German Jewry had seemed so secure. Unlike the Jewry of Eastern Europe, families and communities had been established there for generations. They participated as prosperous burghers in the economic life of the country, and patronized the arts. Nurtured by the seeming permanence, their traditions and customs had time to crystallize and mature. For there was something noble about German Jewry. If in the 19th and 20th centuries Eastern European Jewry looked somewhat askance at their German brethren and questioned their authenticity, yet it was with some degree of awe that they looked askance. The *yekke* was often the object of ridicule — but with an overtone of respect. Germany's seemingly enlightened intellectual climate enabled its Jewish inhabitants to live a dignified and orderly life that was not imaginable in feudal Poland or Russia.

The cultural fruits of this lifestyle are everywhere to be seen, ever since some Lithuanian yeshivah student who developed a taste for secular knowledge first turned his gaze toward Germany. Immigrants from Germany were active in transplanting Jewish life in Western Europe and the New World. The Reform movement, certainly a major development in Jewish history, cannot be discussed without an appraisal of its German origins, and modern Zionism was nourished by its roots in the Haskalah movement, which also originated in Germany.

The present book does not describe the Holocaust at all. That subject is surely one that must be considered separately, though ultimately the demonic forces let loose by Hitler defy human comprehension. What this book does tell, in broad lines, is the story of the origins and growth of German Jewry, its folkways and its communal life, and the major religious and cultural movements that branched out over the whole Jewish world. In this sense, then, this book is a modest memorial to a once glorious community.

1. THE CROSSROADS OF EUROPE

There have been few periods during the past thousand years when Germany was without any Jewish population. Yet visitors to modern Germany will find pitifully few traces of past Jewish life there. Synagogues and schools, houses and hospitals, even cemeteries, were all destroyed during the Hitlerian Holocaust. Those visitors would experience more satisfaction, and certainly less pain, by directing their gaze elsewhere. For German Jewry's claim to historical greatness rests, not on its own longevity, but on the profound contributions which it has made to Jewish life universally. Reform, Conservative, and Neo-Orthodox congregations throughout the western hemisphere; Jewish universities and theological seminaries in Israel and the United States; the great Ashkenazi communities of Eastern Europe and the Russian Pale; each trace their origin and inspiration to Germany. They are the living testimonies to the extraordinary intellectual fecundity of the Jewish communities there. They are also monuments to the diversity of its history.

Part of that diversity must be attributed to the distinctive nature of wider German history. For that, too, is a turbulent story: Throughout the thousand years of Jewish settlement in Germany, the political history of the country underwent violent oscillations of fortune. Even its political boundaries were rarely constant. Ultimately, the Germans were to lay claim to all the territories between the Baltic in the north and the Alps in the south, and between the Rhine in the west and the Oder in the east. Yet this area has never been continuously, exclusively, or wholly German. Indeed in the 10th century, when permanent Jewish settlement began, "Germany" consisted only of the five "stem" *(stamm)* duchies in the west and south. The more easterly marchlands, which in 1945 constituted one-third of the country, were not fully colonized by the Germans until 400

1

The "Old Synagogue" of Essen; photographed early in the century when it was considered one of the most beautiful in Germany.

years later. Even then, however, it was impossible to give any one, definite description of either Germany or the Germans. The borders continued to change drastically, and the nation continued to be one of extremes. In the words of one historian: The Germans "have produced the most transcendental philosophers, the most spiritual musicians, and the most ruthless and unscrupulous politicians." They have dominated almost every cultural current within the continent of which they form the heartland.

"The Synagogue of Ratisbon (Regensburg)," 16th century etchings by Albrecht Altdorfer. The inscription in the vestibule on the etching on the right states that the synagogue was destroyed on February 21, 1519.

Yet they have rarely managed to master themselves. For over a thousand years they failed to recapture the Imperial cohesion established by Charlemagne in the 9th century. The authority of one emperor was replaced by that of numerous princes, one pope by several bishops, one capital by various cities; none strong enough to impose centralization, few weak enough to abandon centrifugalism. Only Hitler truly halted this process. By then, however, Jewish no less than German history had reflected the fact that the country had become the crossroads of violence, as well as of genius, within Europe.

Origins

Our story does not begin until the 9th century. The Jewish communities which were said to have existed in Germany "before the crucifixion" were figments of medieval imaginations. Those which Jewish merchants did establish during the 4th century, in the wake of the conquering Roman legions, were transient. Not until 500 years later did their French and Italian successors decide to settle permanently along western Germany's bustling arteries of international trade. But the decision, once taken, was

An early example of typical Ashkenazi square Hebrew script on an epitaph in Mainz, 1082 c.e.

The entrance to the
11th century *mikveh*
(ritual bath) at
Speyer.

implemented with speed and success. Within a century, such Jewish communities as Mainz on the Rhine and Regensburg on the Danube had proven their commercial capabilities. In 1084 Jews were specifically invited to settle in Speyer by the local Archbishop "in order to enhance a thousandfold the respect accorded to our town" and to make "a city out of the village of Speyer."

Even in this formative period, however, Jewish activity was not restricted to commerce. The cultural tradition which was to make German Jewry famous was already evident. It was, indeed, personified in the leadership of the Kalonymus family, whose combination of financial acumen and intellectual prowess had

The Kalonymus Family

4

already become a byword in Italy. For over 400 years after Kalonymus ben Isaac the Elder had founded the German branch in the 9th century, this family dominated the cultural and political life of the early Rhenish communities. They supplied an array of scholars, preachers, poets, and theologians. They also established standards of learning and leadership which later German Jewry would be proud to emulate.

Persecution and Migration

They were not allowed to do so in peace. On November 26, 1095, Pope Urban II exhorted Christendom to recover the Holy Land from the Moslem infidel. He thus initiated, not only the lavish military adventures known as the Crusades, but also a tale of horror for the Jewish communities which lay along Europe's highway to the East. Zealous in their faith in Jesus, and jealous of the wealth of his supposed murderers, the motley Crusader armies fell upon the Jews before they even encountered the Moslems. Imperial protests, clerical denunciations, and even occasional Jewish reprisals, were equally unavailing. During the summer of 1096 the Crusaders embarked on a bloody rampage which engulfed the communities on the Rhine, and which claimed more than 5,000 Jewish victims.

The Crusades

Some Jews sought immediate refuge in baptism. Far more preferred the eternal salvation of martyrdom. Contemporary chronicles are filled with tales of German Jewish families who followed the ancient example of Hannah and her seven sons. After killing their children (to prevent their forcible baptism) parents willingly took their own lives. The frequency of such actions, and the religious fervor with which they were accomplished, added a new dimension to the traditional concept of *Kiddush ha-Shem* ("Sanctification of the Divine Name"). Martyrdom was no longer an individual act expressing frustration. It now became a collective experience which demonstrated the spiritual strength of a chosen generation of the chosen people. At

Mainz Jews threw their money at their persecutors; not with the object of bribing them, but in order to distract them and thus "buy" the time needed to take their own lives. At Worms, they committed suicide whilst singing psalms. Throughout the region, Abraham's biblical nobility in being willing to sacrifice his son Isaac was constantly recalled. Only in such devotion could German Jewry find comfort. Otherwise, the events of 1096 constitute a chronicle of tragedy. They are known in Jewish history as *Gezerot Tatnav* (the massacres of 4856 a.m. — corresponding to 1096 in the secular calendar).

A 1642 engraving of the plundering of the Frankfort ghetto in 1614.

A Terrible Precedent

Ultimately, German Jewish life was resumed; the destroyed communities of Worms, Speyer, Metz, and Cologne were rebuilt, and others (Breslau in 1203 and Berlin in 1295) were founded in the formerly Slav territories which the Germans had themselves begun colonizing in the East. But the psychological damage of the Crusades proved to be of longer duration. A terrible precedent had been set. Jewish lives were no longer inviolable; in times of

6

social or religious ferment they would be at the mercy of the disorderly mob. The relative calm of the second and third Crusades (12th century) was therefore deceptive. An anti-Jewish folk tradition, as expressed in the mystery plays, had already been established. Hereafter, medieval German history is punctuated by a bewildering turmoil of slaughter and outrage. The pretexts were largely irrelevant. Charges that Jews had murdered Christian children (as in Fulda in 1235), that they had prevented one of their number from adopting Christianity (as in Frankfort in 1241), or that they had desecrated the Host (as in Munich in 1285), were equally good excuses for murderous riots and immediate expulsion. Roving gangs of ruffians, such as those led by the Jew-baiter Rindfleisch in Franconia in 1298, could destroy entire communities with impunity. No wonder that by that year one German rabbi feared that soon not one Jew would be left in all Germany.

The seeds which had been sown in 1096 bore their most *Black Death* tragic fruit between 1348 and 1350, the years of the Black

The *Yizkor* (Memorial) prayer from the *memorbuch* of the Coblenz community, commemorating the communities destroyed during the persecutions of 1349.

Death. Europe was ravaged by an epidemic of various diseases which claimed between one quarter and one half of its total population, the greatest scourge of its kind in recorded history. No one could discover a medical explanation, few even made the attempt. Most Germans, especially, were convinced that their troubles had been caused by the Jews, who had poisoned the wells. This charge was ridiculed by both Pope and Emperor, it was denied by the Jews, and it was disproved by Jewish losses during the epidemic. Nevertheless, on this pretext over 300 German Jewish communities were destroyed, often in anticipation of the plague rather than as a result of an actual visitation. Only the political disunity of Germany prevented a general decree of expulsion; instead, when the Jews were driven out of one district they were usually able to buy refuge in another. Meanwhile, however, the axis of Jewish settlement in northern Europe inexorably moved eastwards away from the Rhineland, towards Poland and Russia.

The tragedy of attack from without was exacerbated by the *Pfefferkorn-* tribulation of denigration from within. In 1507, one Johannes *Reuchlin* Pfefferkorn (1469-after 1521), a Jewish butcher from Cologne who had embraced Christianity in order to avoid a charge of common theft, published a series of scurrilous pamphlets against his former faith. Despite, or perhaps because of, his ignorance of the Talmud, Pfefferkorn concentrated his venom on that work. By 1509, after exploiting the patronage of the Cologne Dominicans and utilizing the piety of the Emperor's sister, he had secured Imperial permission to suppress its study in Frankfort, Mainz, and other German cities. The zeal with which Pfefferkorn set to work shocked the Jews. It also scandalized the growing body of Christian humanists, and thus led to the greatest "battle of books" that Europe had ever known. For a decade Johannes Reuchlin (1455-1522), one of the most renowned Christian German scholars of the day, answered Pfefferkorn pamphlet for pamphlet, invective for invective, and charge for charge. Yet, his

Abb. 52. Titelblatt zu: Pfefferkorn, Der Juden Feind. Augsburg 1509.

Title page from the apostate Pfefferkorn's tract, *Der Juden Feind*, Augsburg, 1509.

brilliant defence of Jewish literature and rabbinics was unavailing. In 1520 the Pope ruled in Pfefferkorn's favor; even before then, in 1519, the Jews of Regensburg had been banished for failing to comply with his orders.

Continuity and Change

On October 31, 1517, a moody Augustinian friar named Martin Luther (1483-1546) nailed 95 theses against Catholicism to the door of the Wittenberg church. To European Christendom this action heralded the spiritual ferment known as the Protestant Reformation. To German Jewry it seemd a prelude to yet another physical trial; for they became the sport of opposing religious factions, and were trapped by the ensuing antagonism of

Martin Luther

9

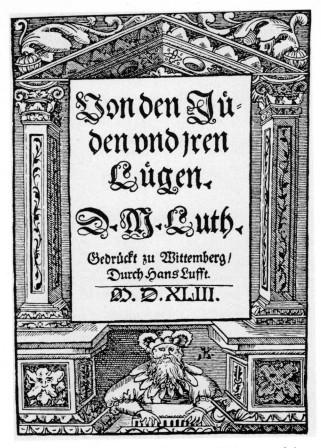

Concerning the Jews and Their Lies. Title page of the most virulent of Luther's anti-Semitic pamphlets, advising the princes to "drive the lazy bones out of our system." Wittenberg, 1543.

political enemies who supported, or opposed, Luther's movement for their own ends. In this trial of strength between Pope and Protestant, Emperor and princes, estates and burgesses which

10

split Germany asunder, there appeared no refuge for the Jews. Luther himself, who initially sympathized with their refusal to convert to "papal paganism," ultimately became enraged with their rejection of even his purified Protestantism. The Catholics, convinced of Jewry's responsibility for Luther's movement, were only slightly less vitriolic. Luther exhorted his followers to burn synagogues and banish the Jews. Revived Catholicism (in a movement known as the Counter Reformation) insisted on their humiliation. Wherever the papal writ ran, the Talmud was vilified, ghettos were further restricted, and Jews were forced to wear a distinctive yellow hat.

Yet for all the tragedies which it brought upon German Jewry, the Reformation eventually benefited individual German Jews. In Protestant territories for instance (where the doctrine of transubstantiation was denied), Jews could no longer be accused of desecrating the Host. Instead, because Protestantism emphasized the importance of Hebrew, ancient Hebrew laws and values were now likely to be (and by many sects were) afforded equal respect. Even Catholic princes, after thirty years of inconclusive religious warfare, in 1648 finally accepted the impossibility of imposing their orthodoxy throughout the continent. In so doing, they too reluctantly acknowledged the principle of toleration. Admittedly the Germans, unlike the English and the Dutch, did not immediately implement this ideal. But their princes did exploit it for their own ends.

These men were determined to repair the physical devastation of the religious wars, and were prepared to employ any section of the new "capitalist" class — including the Jews — to help them do so. Expansion, enrichment, and efficiency were their watchwords. They therefore regarded the faith of a Jew as far less important than his economic and administrative worth. It was thus that these so-called "absolutist" princes, who by the 18th century were common throughout Germany, took a remarkable psychological step forward. Instead of looking at an indistinguishable, and unpalatable, collective mass of Jewry, they measured the worth of individual Jews. Of course these enlightened despots, notwithstanding their devotion to "reason," still unreasonably detested the Jewish people *en masse*. But if they thought that an individual member of the faith might prove serviceable, then they would grant him grudging toleration.

Jews receiving a charter of privileges from Emperor Henry VII in 1312. The Jews are wearing distinctive pointed hats.

Frederick the Great of Prussia (1712-1786), the architect of one of the most efficient and successful military administrations of the century, illustrates this ambivalence perfectly. He despised his Jewish subjects as a group; subjecting them to a degrading poll tax, limiting the number of their offspring, and even forcing them to buy a specified quantity of porcelain from the royal

Frederick the Great

12

factory. But while thus making life miserable for the mass, Frederick was perfectly capable of sublimating his prejudices and being gracious to a few. Successful traders, skilled administrators, all those who could be used as court purveyors or financiers, became "privileged" Jews. They were allowed a host of bounties and concessions which included the right to mix freely with their gentile neighbors, and even to reside amongst them. The majority of Prussian Jewry (and Prussia's Jewish population was later to be vastly increased by the partitions of Poland in 1793 and 1795) remained herded within the ghetto. But there were significant numbers outside it, not only in Prussia but in Frankfort, Dresden, Leipzig, Kassel, Brunswick, Halle, and Westphalia too.

Emancipation and Rejection

Unwittingly, the needs of the absolutists thus paved the way for the emancipation of the Jews. The first generation of privileged Jews gained commercial and communal power. Their sons gained more; regular contact with secular society and full participation in its "enlightened" civilization. The daughters went even further; for it was they who often found it easiest to become culturally and socially assimilated in Germany. The beauty, wit, and vivacity of such Jewesses as Henrietta Herz (1764-1847) and Rachel Varnhagen (1771-1833) made their cultural salons the most brilliant in Berlin. They also created a certain type of Jew acceptable to the intellectual and artistic amongst Christian German society. By the time Gotthold Ephraim Lessing (1729-1781) — the first modern Christian dramatist to portray a Jew in sympathetic terms — wrote his play *Nathan the Wise* (1779), some Germans were acknowledging the right of individual Jews to be treated as human beings. They were still selective in their friendships, but they were no longer indiscriminate in their prejudices.

This first flush of warmth was not allowed to develop naturally. Neither was Jewish emancipation in Germany per-

Napoleon

13

mitted to follow a quiet progression, whereby the Germans might voluntarily have agreed to this course. Instead, they were driven to it in the early 19th century at the point of a bayonet. Worse still, that bayonet was in the hands of a foreigner, in the person of Napoleon's conquering grenadier. It was the French who battered down the ghetto walls in Germany, they who enforced the constitutional equality of its emancipated denizens, and they who welcomed Jewish commercial initiative throughout the duchies they occupied. Even in Prussia, where emancipation accompanied a reforming program undertaken without direct French intervention in 1812, it had been prompted by the crushing defeat at Jena in 1807.

In the long term, this proved disastrous for the German Jews. Because their emancipation was accompanied by the humiliation of German arms, they were explicitly associated with defeat and the foreigner. A wave of emergent Tuetomania swept Germany after Napoleon's defeat in 1815. In its course it swept aside all the edicts of Jewish emancipation which he had granted. This romantic chauvinism did not preclude extensive Jewish participation in Germany's flourishing industry and commerce. Long before the first world war much of the community was highly prosperous. Neither did it prevent some German Jews from attaining political fame. It was in Germany that Ferdinand Lassalle (1825-1864), whose life was prematurely ended in a duel over a baroness, became head of the most powerful trade union in the world. But it did imply Jewish exclusion from the patriarchal state and conservative constitution which appeared natural to the German spirit and past. As early as August 1819 an assortment of nationalist students, romantic writers, and unemployed farmhands had attacked Jews throughout Germany. Their cries of "Hep! Hep!" once an exhortation to domestic animals, announced the first onslaught of modern popular anti-Semitism. With the triumph of German conservatism after the unification of the Reich in 1870, such outbreaks became common. Not even

14

A contemporary print of the "Hep! Hep!" riots, 1819.

Bismarck (1815-1898), the Iron Chancellor who entrusted his
own fortune to Jewish bankers, could ignore such feelings. He
did, in 1870, proclaim Jewish emancipation throughout Germany. Yet the legal code still precluded Jewish participation in
the government, whilst national custom also excluded Jews from
army commissions and university chairs.

For only two fleeting moments between 1815 and 1933 did *Liberal*
German Jewry appear free from this anti-Semitic shadow. The *Interludes*
first occurred in 1848; suddenly, a national cry for liberalism and
unity drowned the echoes of ancient antagonisms. Seven Jews
were invited to the parliament assembled at Frankfort to draft a
national constitution. Numerous others were acclaimed at politi-

16

A lithograph of the "Old Synagogue" in Frankfort. The men on the left are reciting *Kiddush Levanah,* the blessing over the new moon.

cal congresses and demonstrations elsewhere. Just 70 years later, with the birth of the Weimar Republic in 1918, a similar (albeit more muted) scene took place. One Jew, Hugo Preuss (1860-1925), drafted the new constitution; another, Walter Rathenau (1867-1922), became the first minister of reconstruction. Yet both events proved aberrations. The liberal intellectuals of 1848 were soon put to flight by the forces of reaction. Many were forced into permanent exile. Those of 1918, although they retained a semblance of power somewhat longer, suffered a far worse fate.

Assimilation and Nationalism

No German Jew in the 19th century could possibly have foreseen the lengths to which anti-Semitism would go. Many, indeed, did emigrate. United States Jewry, particularly during the 1860s, frequently spoke English with a German accent, when it was not speaking its native German. But many others admired, even loved, the very idea which was working to exclude them from German society, that of the Tuetonic Fatherland. For instance, those members of the Convention of German Jewish Students (founded in 1896) who proclaimed their equality with their German brothers by out-drinking, out-cursing, and out-duelling them, also protested their loyalty to Germany by denying Jewish national separatism. Their viewpoint had been articulated as early as 1848 by Gabriel Riesser (1806-1863), the Jewish vice-president of the Frankfort parliament. Ever since being debarred from practicing as a notary because of his faith, Riesser had devoted his considerable literary and debating skills to the struggle for Jewish emancipation. The liberal delegates at Frankfort, in a genuine display of sympathy, offered to realize this aim by making "the peculiar condition of the Israelitish race" the object of special legislation. But Riesser leapt to his feet in protest. The Jews, he objected, were neither a separate race nor a nation; as "Germans of the Jewish faith" they should merely be

Germans of the Jewish Faith

Gabriel Riesser

17

included in a general statement of equal rights applicable to all Germans.

Riesser, although he did abandon the observance of Judaism in private life, never formally denied his faith in public. In this he differed from many of his Jewish contemporaries. Some had been genuinely attracted to Christian culture, and despised the Jewish counterpart as barren and primitive. Far more had cynically accepted apostasy as a ticket to professional and economic advancement. Heinrich Heine (1797-1856), the great German *Heinrich Hei*

The yellow badge worn by this 16th century German Jew was in the shape of a circle (left). Suesskind von Trimberg depicted in an early 14th century manuscript. Note the pointed Jew's hat (below).

lyric poet, was such a case. To the end of his days he never lost his revulsion for Christianity nor his respect for ancient Judaism. Yet this had not prevented his swift conversion to the former in 1825, when he felt that he could strike a social bargain by doing so. As he put it: "If I could have made a living by stealing silver spoons without going to prison, I would never have been christened."

Whichever the case, between the time of Frederick the Great's death and Hitler's rise to power, assimilation and apostasy had almost assumed the dimensions of mass movements amongst German Jews. Even by the mid-19th century, most of the wealthy and educated amongst them had been lost by conversion. By 1933 the process had extended further down the social scale. The Jewish population of Germany rose from 512,158 in 1871 to 615,021 by 1910, but showed no natural increase after that date. It is a tribute to the strength of the community that, as we shall see, it was still capable of outstanding contributions to Jewish culture. Nor must the picture be exaggerated. There were many who proclaimed their identity by joining the Zionist movement, and many who practiced their faith with deep orthodoxy. But what has to be recorded is that after 1918 the numbers of German Jewry were maintained only by the steady flow of refugees from Eastern Europe.

Assimilation and Apostasy

2. THE ASHKENAZIM

Origins

In medieval times, German Jews would probably have described their contemporary co-religionists in Spain as Sephardim. The latter, conversely, would have identified German Jews as Ashkenazim. Originally, both generic terms were specifically geographical descriptions, derived from the Hebrew *Sepharad* and *Ashkenaz* (which had come to mean Spain and Germany respectively). But their meaning was always far wider. These terms indi-

The Term

19

A Ḥanukkah *menorah* for oil; Frankfort, early 18th century. The ornamentation on the stems is reminiscent of that in the Temple candelabrum.

cated, not so much the country in which a particular Jew lived, as the Jewish cultural complex to which he belonged. This is even more so today. The geographical origins of the two cultural traditions have largely become irrelevant. The Sephardi influence, for instance, had undergone a shift of axis from Spain to North Africa, the Middle East, and Latin America. The Askhenazi heritage, too, has been carried far beyond its original confines. The *Yekkes* German Jews, specifically, are no longer referred to as Ashkenazim, but rather derogatorily as *yekkes;* a term which reflected the surprise felt by East European Jews on seeing their German coreligionists abandon the traditional long frock-coat for the modern short jacket (German, *Jacke*). Neither is German Jewry

20

now the major guardian over the cultural heritage of their forbears. The main spheres of Ashkenazi influence are Eastern Europe, the United States, and the lands which once comprised the British Empire. Modern Israel contains significant numbers of both groups.

This transformation was not anticipated by the earliest German Jews. They had intended, not to pioneer a new cultural tradition, but to preserve their ancient heritage, which had been born in Roman Palestine and fostered in medieval Italy. Admittedly, their religious habits did already differ in some minor respects from those of their Spanish brethren. But this was often because the latter had inherited their customs from that other

A velvet embroidered *parokhet* (curtain for the synagogue ark), dated 1744 and used in the Kassel synagogue. It was made by a woman on the occasion of the *bar mitzvah* of her son.

21

cradle of rabbinic Judaism, Talmudic Babylon. Even until as late as the 12th century the very word *Ashkenaz* retained its strictly biblical meaning, and referred to some part of the Middle East. It was not applied to Germany until it was heard to bear a certain phonic resemblance to the word "Saxon," the predominant local element whom the first Jews met there. Not until the 14th century did *Ashkenaz* denote a distinct cultural entity; as different from *Sepharad* as was Germany from Spain.

Thereafter the gap widened. The ghetto which the German authorities built to keep their Jews in, also served Judaism in that it kept external influences out. Segregation was often preferred, even when it was not enforced. Within their secluded settlements the Jews of Germany could not only preserve the religion of their ancestors; they could also develop cultural characteristics of their own. The human individuality of idiosyncratic Ashkenazim was not thereby submerged. Indeed in Frankfort, for example, it was deliberately preserved by hanging separate signs over certain houses; and it was from those red shields, eagles, or ships that the Rothschilds, Adlers, and Schiffs derived their famous family names. But the unique circumstances of the group nevertheless endowed the Ashkenazim, as a whole, with social and religious characteristics which made them clearly distinguishable from the Sephardim, and which much of later Jewry elsewhere subsequently adopted.

Liturgy

The Ashkenazi liturgy was one sphere in which a distinctive development was clearly apparent. Jews in Germany, whilst addressing their Maker in the same basic form and prayers as those in Spain, could not help reminding Him of the unique trials which they had undergone. Few German congregations did not retain (and unfortunately revise) their *memorbuchen* — lists of local martyrs which were declaimed in the synagogues on appropriate Sabbaths. Even fewer communities neglected to include in

Wall painting, 1733, in the Bavarian synagogue of Bechhofen, containing various private prayers. The synagogue was restored in 1914 by the Bavarian Commission for National Art Treasures, but was destroyed by the Nazis.

their liturgies the numerous penitential prayers *(selihot)*, devotional poems *(piyyutim)*, and laments *(kinot)* which glorified the self-sacrifice of their massacred forbears during the Crusades and Black Death. No German community could ever feel completely safe from attack. Their rabbis therefore lengthened the conclusion of the Friday evening service to save latecomers from having to walk home alone in the dark.

Later Eastern European communities somewhat altered the Ashkenazi prayerbook, substituting "Polish" for "Rhineland" usages. But it has retained the scars of its German origins. According to legend, it is to a German martyr of the 10th century, for instance, that the High Holy Day services owe one of *Amnon of Mainz*

their most beautiful and hallowed sections. The *U-Netanneh Tokef* prayer, which epitomizes the sublime notion of the Day of Judgement, is said to have been composed by Amnon of Mainz. He first uttered it in a German synagogue, whence he had been carried after withstanding the most extreme tortures in defence of his faith. To this day it is, therefore, recited during the Additional service *(Musaf)* on the New Year (and also, according to the Polish rite, on the Day of Atonement).

Silver charity box, Halberstadt, Germany, 1761.
It bears the inscription, taken from Proverbs 21:14:
"A gift in secret pacifies anger." The box was used
for collections in the synagogue.

Lore

In general, medieval German Jewry was renowned for the strin- *Religious Law* gency and pedantry with which it performed religious precepts.

No wonder therefore that Asher ben Yeḥiel (known by his acronym "Rosh"; 1250-1327), a leading German rabbi whom persecution forced to flee to Spain, found much to criticize in the country of his adoption. Yet the hostile environment had dictated changes in the religious orthodoxy even of German Jewry. Fear of derision by the gentile populace, for instance, forced German rabbis to permit the wearing of shoes in public on the ninth of Av, a day of national mourning. The specter of

A page from the *Erna Michael Haggadah,* Middle Rhine, c. 1400. The stylized floral scrolls, dragons, and architectural structures are typical of the Rhineland area illuminated manuscripts.

The *bet ha-midrash* adjoining the Old Synagogue of Worms, which is said
to contain the seat on which Rashi studied. Photographed before 1938 (above).
The interior of the Worms synagogue (below).

destitution induced them to permit those trading in viticulture to benefit from wine handled by non-Jews. The irregularity of sustenance spurred them to heights of ingenuity unknown in Spain when deriving a formula for the fictitious sale of leavened foods before Passover. And the danger of mob attack on Christmas Eve (known in Yiddish as *nittel*, from *Natale Domini* — Latin, "The birth of our Lord") drove them to rule that Jews even abandon the study of the sacred law on that occasion, and quietly play cards instead.

Not that life in the ghetto was uniformly miserable. Indeed, *Aesthetics* the Jews of Germany took particular pains to ensure that their spirits would not be dampened. They compensated for the lack of color in their lives by a brilliant display of finery on their festivals. They gave vent to their frustrated artistic imaginations by an array of synagogue decorations and by intricate illuminations of their sacred manuscripts. Young men found an outlet for their energies in jousts on the Christian model whilst sympathetic rabbis looked for every possible means of preserving the more mundane joys of daily life. Jacob ben Moses Moellin of Mainz ("Maharil"; ?1360-1427), for instance, permitted "placing tree branches in water on the Sabbath . . . in order to provide a source of joy for the house"; when asked about celebrating a wedding in a community where a local ordinance forbade the making of music, the same rabbi ordered that the event be moved elsewhere, rather than have the bride and bridegroom forego the pleasure.

In their search for compensatory outlets, the German Jews *Outside* even resorted to occasional borrowings from their Gentile sur- *Influence* roundings. Despite the bitterness which characterized so many German-Jewish relationships, contact between them could nevertheless often be intimate. Before 1096, especially, "practically every Jew was in direct contact with his non-Jewish neighbors, depending on them for earning his living, for manual labor, and for personal services." Thus synagogue architecture aped the severe Gothic style of the local churches. Indeed, both the Worms synagogue and the Friedburg ritual bath *(mikveh)* were designed by the creators of the Christian places of worship in those towns. Synagogue melodies, similarly, echoed medieval German folk music, from which festival and Sabbath table songs borrowed freely. The popular *Ḥad Gadya* ("One Kid") rhyme, for instance, with which Ashkenazim still conclude the Passover *seder* service, is based on a 16th century German song. Neither were German Jews immune to the rife superstition of their gentile neighbors. *Wachnacht,* guarding a baby boy against demons the night before his circumcision, owed its origin to this influence.

Title page of a *minhagim* book printed in Berlin, which includes the customs of the communities of Poland, Lithuania and Germany, among others, 1703.

28

As early as the 12th century, some German rabbis had begun transcribing compilations of such distinctive local customs. Whilst many of their works served merely to fire local patriotism (as in the case of the famous Frankfort *minhag* books), others became the basis for future Ashkenazi practice. Thus the customs followed by Meir ben Baruch of Rothenburg ("Maharam"; c. 1215-1293), and even the liturgical tunes, known as *Mi-Sinai* melodies, attributed to Jacob ben Moses Moellin, became virtually sacrosanct.

Moreover, although many German traditions were passing *Universal* phases, several others became permanent features of Ashkenazi *Custom* Jewry. Marriage rites are a case in point. It was in Germany that Jewish bridegrooms first became generally accustomed to crush a glass underfoot during their wedding ceremony; there that traditional Jewish matchmakers *(shadkhanim)* first enjoyed respect and prestige; and there that monogamy, having become general practice, first attained the sanction of Jewish law. At the opposite scale of human emotions, German Jews also initiated the practice of lighting a candle on the anniversary of a relative's death. Their word for the occasion, *yahrzeit,* was even adopted by some Sephardim.

Language

The language of German Jews was equally distinctive. The *Yiddish* learned, traditionally, retained the use of Hebrew-Aramaic in written communications. The enlightened, increasingly, adopted the vernacular. But the majority very quickly developed a unique jargon of their own. Exposed to several varieties of Christian German, the new arrivals from Italy and France adopted elements from numerous dialects, and thereby gave birth to the Yiddish language. In some instances (e.g. *bentshn* – "to bless" from "benedicere") they retained traces of their Romance origins. In others they merely copied, and thereby preserved, local German vocabulary *(schwer-* "father-in-law" is unknown in

any other language). In others still, they reached back into the
ancient Hebrew texts.

A wedding, 18th century, Germany. The ceremony takes
place in the open, under a portable canopy. On the butt-
ress of the synagogue is a *traustein,* the "marriage stone,"
against which the bridegroom broke the traditional glass
in remembrance of the destruction of Jerusalem.

Yiddish literature soon followed. Translations of the Bible in *Literature*
the 12th century, of prayer books in the 15th, and of popular
rabbinic legends in the 16th, were all interspersed with innumerable Purim plays, *tkhines* (private devotional prayers for women),

and long narrative poems compiled, in the contemporary German fashion, to commemorate current events. Not all of this literature is of purely semantic interest. The Yiddish memoirs by Glueckel of Hameln (1645-1724), a perceptive Jewess who spent her life amongst the communities of northern Germany, were specifically written as historical records for her descendants. They record the age of her marriage (14), the detailed financial advice with which she plied her husband, the manner in which she raised 12 children whilst doing so, and even the prayers which she recited after his death. Glueckel, who took 28 years over this work, has left us with an idea, not only of the Yiddish language which her contemporaries spoke, but also of the life they led.

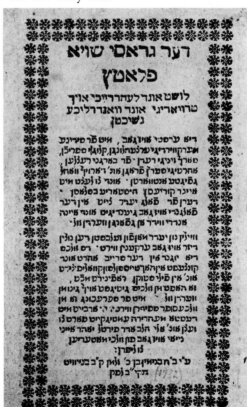

Title page of *Der Grosse Shoi Platz* ("The Great Show Place," Neuwied, 1752); first edition of a Yiddish periodical that promised to appear as a bi-annual or quarterly.

31

Yiddish did not, of course, remain an exclusively German
Jewish tongue. It was taken eastwards during the medieval
period, and by the 19th century the vast majority of Yiddish
speakers had never set foot on German soil. By then, however,
even their Hebrew pronunciation had been influenced by their
German ancestors. Some of the differences between what is now
termed the Sephardi and Ashkenazi pronunciations may possibly
be traced to different dialects common in Babylon and Palestine.
But the emergence of a distinctive Ashkenazi accent in Central
Europe no earlier than the 13th century cannot be related solely
to this cause. It was, rather, the Yiddish vowel system of that
period which probably caused German Jews to transfer similar
sound shifts to the sacred tongue.

Learning

Whilst their liturgy, lore, and language made German Jews
distinct, it was their tradition of learning which gave them distinction. Their history, even during its bleakest period, is punctuated with the names of masters of Jewish scholarship. Their
society, whatever its circumstances, ensured that the tradition
was not entrusted solely to the erudite, or wealthy few. Every
Jewish boy and girl was taught the rudiments of the Holy Language, as well as the fundamentals of the faith. Indeed, universal
elementary education was the norm amongst Jewish communities
at a time when it was unheard of in other contemporary groups.
In isolated settlements private tutors were employed to meet the
need; in major centers *yeshivot,* higher academies of learning,
were designed to satisfy the demand. A child's first day at school
(*heder* — "room") was a major family celebration, sweetened by
generous helpings of honey and cake. A community's completion
of a talmudic tractate became a minor festive occasion *(siyyum).*
At all times, German Jews looked to their texts, not merely for
guidance, but also as an escape. Immersed in those pages they
would forget the bitterness of the world around them, and by

"Friday Evening" by Moritz Oppenheim. On returning home from the synagogue the father of this prosperous German Jewish household blesses his daughters with the traditional formula, "May God make thee like Sarah, Rebekah, Rachel and Leah." The sons await their turn. The figure on the right may be a yeshivah student invited for the Sabbath meal. Note the "Sabbath lamp" in the shape of a star suspended over the table.

poring over them find rest for their souls, which cruel fate so often tortured.

Study of the law was not, of course, restricted to the Jews of Germany. This religious precept was equally binding on the Sephardim, and equally honored by them. Yet even here the two groups differed. The Sephardi methods were those of condensation, systematization, and philosophical synthesis; their interests were poetry, grammar, and the Bible, as well as the Talmud. German Jews made different demands. They required their teachers to teach, not speculate, and their scholars to elucidate, not condense. For them the Talmud was supreme, and it was they who, in medieval times, helped to revolutionize its study.

Their starting point was the commentary of the Talmud *Tosafists* written in the 11th century by Rashi (as he is known from the initials of his title and name, Rabbi Shelomo Yitzḥaki; 1040-1105), the great French scholar and one-time student in Mainz. His monumental work, although indispensable, was not exhaustive. It was embellished by numerous *tosafot* (additions) compiled by scores of keen-witted students who, in the *yeshivot* of France and Germany, cavilled their way through tortuous talmudic byways in search of answers to their questions. Even their opinions were neither unanimous nor final. But their methodology became standard. From the clustered cities along the Rhine, the *tosafist* tradition of minute examination and exacting enquiry spread to Spain, Eastern Europe, and England. It facilitated the novellae *(hiddushim)* which were to become the standard tools of the rabbi's trade. It encouraged a form of subtle casuistry known as *pilpul* ("pepper"), which became a craze during the 16th and 17th centuries. Above all, it confirmed the position of the Talmud as the basic text of Jewish learning.

The *tosafist* tradition originated in France, amongst Rashi's grandchildren and it was there that it reached its apogee. But once carried to Speyer by Isaac ben Asher ha-Levi ("Riba"; late

34

11th-early 12th century), it found some of its greatest exponents amongst German Jewry. In Worms there was Eliezer ben Judah (c. 1165-1230), renowned for his ability to explain complete biblical sentences by the numerical value of their individual letters *(gematriya)*; in Cologne, Eliezer ben Joel ha-Levi ("Ravya"; 1140-1225), "the pillar of decision and the foundation of *halakhah";* in Regensburg, Ephraim ben Isaac (1110-1175), who "never conceded a point"; and in Rothenburg, the great Meir ben Baruch. The differences between them were quantitative, not qualitative. Overriding their varying number of pupils or novellae were their common heights of intellectual achievement. Under the influence of the *tosafists,* talmudic scholarship, always venerated, now became exalted. They combined sublime faith in the intrinsic sanctity of the work with a critical analysis of its apparent inconsistencies. Their comments, together with those of Rashi, are now permanent features of every printed page of the Talmud, and constitute the outer margin of the standard texts. They have thus become the symbol of the degree to which the *tosafists* enriched the tradition of Jewish learning, and of the extent to which they enhanced the greatness of their community.

Under any circumstances it would have been difficult to maintain these standards of talmudic scholarship. In the conditions prevailing in late medieval Germany it was impossible. Thereafter, Eastern Europe claimed hegemony in this field. Meir ben Baruch ha-Levi (died in 1404), Israel ben Ḥayyim Bruna (c.1400-1480), and Moses Mintz (15th century), although renowned halakhic authorities, did not emulate the learning of their predecessors in Germany. Only in 1622, when a child prodigy named Meir Schiff ("Maharam"; 1605-1641) was appointed rabbi of Fulda, did talmudic scholarship really begin to revive there. Subsequently however, not even the tragic brevity of Schiff's life broke the chain. Further links were provided by Jair Bacharach (1638-1702), whose exhaustive knowl-

Later Sages

35

edge of general science matched his monumental talmudic expertise; by Zevi Hirsch Ashkenazi of Altona ("Ḥakham Zevi"; 1660-1718), whose carefully constructed responsa belied a stormy life which carried him as far east as Russia and as far west as London; by Ashkenazi's brilliant son, Jacob Emden, to whom we shall return and by Phineḥas ben Zevi Hirsch ha-Levi Horowitz (1730-1805), the saintly and scholarly rabbi of Frankfort, whose family was to furnish European Jewry with many

Zevi Hirsch Ashkenazi, one of the most important halakhic authorities of his day.

Akiva Eger, rabbi of Posen, a posthumous portrait
by Constalt.

generations of spiritual leaders. Sometimes, communal scholarship benefited from personal tragedy. Jacob Falk (1680-1756),
for instance, lost all his family in a gunpowder explosion in
Poland. His subsequent vow to devote himself to study brought
immediate benefit to the communities of Berlin, Metz, and
Frankfort, where he taught. On other occasions, wealth eased the
path of honor. Thus the prodigious natural talents of Akiva Eger
(1761-1837), one of the greatest halakhic authorities of his age,

were carefully nurtured in the comfortable home of his wealthy father-in-law.

The revival in German-Jewish scholarship coincided with a *Printing* flowering of German-Jewish printing. The first Hebrew presses in Germany had been established during the early 16th century (at Tuebingen in 1511, at Frankfort in 1512, and at Cologne in 1518). But it was not until the influx of Polish Jews, in the wake of the Chmielnicki massacres in the 17th century, that the demand for copies of the Talmud, prayerbooks, and devotional literature grew to significant proportions in Germany. By the 18th century, however, Hebrew printing had become a profitable business, as well as a pious enterprise. It was then that German publishing houses, many of them owned by Christian "front" companies, made their great contribution to Jewish scholarship. Their products became renowned for their clarity and for their standards of accuracy, and were often the first authentic texts of their kind. Thus, the Frankfort Talmud (1720-1723), became the basis for all future standard editions, whilst Wolf Heidenheim's (1757-1832) 9-volume edition of the festival prayer book (*maḥzor; Sefer Kerovot,* Roedelheim, 1800), contained the first pure German translation of the liturgical poems for the festivals. His daily prayer book (*siddur; Safah Berurah,* 1806) was, in the course of time, accepted as a standard Ashkenazi version, as was Seligman Isaac Baer's (1825-1897) *Avodat Yisrael* (Roedelheim, 1868). Indeed in many instances, the clear Roedelheim texts were still being reproduced over 100 years later.

Long before then, however, German Jewry's scholastic tradi- *Haskalah* tion had begun to take a revolutionary course. By the end of the 18th century, many enlightened and educated minds in Germany rejected the traditional study of the Talmud as the only key to Jewish values. They sought, instead, to arrive at a rational assessment of Judaism by subjecting it to the accepted European discipline of historical criticism, which increasing numbers of German Jews were being taught at German universities. Their

38

motives, moreover, were as modern as their methods. Through historical research they planned to recapture the pristine Judaism of the past. By scientific investigation they wished to combat the anti-Jewish prejudices of the present. And through a cultured presentation of Judaism in all its historic and moral splendor, they aspired to facilitate the emancipation of Jewry in the future. Their efforts opened fields of study which are still being profitably pursued today.

"The Science of Judaism" *(Wissenschaft des Judentums)*, as *Wissenschaft* this particular form of study became known, was not confined to

Title page of the tractate *Bekhorot* from the Babylonian Talmud, printed in Frankfort, 1720, by the non-Jew Johann Koelner. It bears the Hapsburg double-headed eagle in an escutcheon (left). Title page of *Zina David,* on the laws of porging, printed in Fuerth, 1750. The figures represent Moses wielding a rod and Aaron dressed in the High Priest's robes and holding an incense burner (right).

עם פירוש רש"י ותוספות ופסקי תוספות ופירוש המשניות
מהרמב"ם זצ"ל

Cum Privil. Cæfar. Majeft.

בפרנקפורט דמיין

Germany. Amongst its earliest adherents were S.D. Luzatto ("Shadal"; 1800-1865) in Italy, N. Krochmal ("Ranak"; 1785-1840) in Galicia, and S. Rapoport ("Shir"; 1790-1867) in Prague. But its inspirational pioneers were predominantly Germans, members of the community which was not only the largest in western Europe but also, by virtue of its geographical location, probably the most sensitive to the new ideologies sweeping the continent. They were led, and to a degree personified, by *Leopold Zunz* Leopold Zunz (1794-1886). Sheer will power and brilliance had enabled this child of an orphanage to win acceptance to Berlin University. Scholastic achievements of a supreme nature were to ensure him prominence in every area which he studied. When only 27 Zunz had conceived a detailed plan for the study and evaluation of all Jewish literature. After also outlining the novel methods by which this massive research would be accomplished, he later went on to complete most of the task single-handed. His revolutionary combination of minute research and novel analysis is nicely illustrated in his little book on Rashi. He was the first to use Rashi's own works to obtain a picture, not only of the man

Leopold Zunz, one of the outstanding scholars of the historical school of Jewish studies.

40

The synagogue at Worms, reconstructed in 1961 from the 11th century building destroyed by the Nazis in 1938. The smaller building to the right is the "Rashi Chapel".

The tombstones of Meir ben Baruch — the Maharam of Rothenburg, and Rabbi Alexander of Wimpen in the Jewish cemetery in Worms.

A pewter Ḥanukkah lamp from Horb, Germany, 18th century.

Part of the barrel vault of the synagogue in Horb. The wooden synagogue was decorated and painted by Eliezer Sussman in 1735. Among the various religious symbols Jerusalem is depicted. The synagogue has been reconstructed at the Israel Museum in Jerusalem.

himself, but also of his environment, his family, and even his library.

Zunz's example was followed, in other fields, by his equally distinguished disciples. Thus, the scholarly caution and intellectual flair of Zacharias Frankel and Abraham Geiger (see page 53) transformed the study of Jewish law and of the Hebrew language, respectively. They were joined, still in this first generation, by Moritz Steinschneider (1816-1907), a Moravian Jew who had *Moritz* received a thorough secular education at the universities of *Steinschneider* Vienna and Berlin. His monumental catalogues of the Hebrew books and manuscripts in five major European libraries (Oxford, Leiden, Munich, Hamburg and Berlin), were the first of their kind and are still essential to scholars. They earned him fame as "the father of Jewish bibliography," and reward with an honorary professorship from the Prussian government. But if Steinschneider thus made the Science of Judaism respected, it was Heinrich Graetz (1817-1891), professor of history at Breslau University, who made it popular. His 11 volume *History of the Jews* (yet another first) is still read, not only for its scholarship, but also for its felicitous literary style.

The achievements of these early scholars is all the more *Institutions* remarkable in that they largely had to work under conditions of *of Higher* financial insecurity if not poverty. Their contribution to Jewish *Learning* studies was consequently made all the greater by their farsighted determination that their pupils would study within a more established, and institutionalized, atmosphere. By the end of the 19th century almost all their hopes were already fulfilled. In its second generation, the Science of Judaism was taught in recognized seminaries and disseminated by a range of such learned periodicals as the *Monatschrifft fuer Geschichte und Wissenschaft des Judentums* (1851-1939). Its research was supported by various institutions devoted to Jewish literature, history, and statistics and was published in a series of monographs by the Mekize Nirdamim Society (founded 1864). Of all these achievements, the first was probably the most important. Zunz, in 1848, had failed to obtain a Jewish Studies faculty at Berlin University. But Frankel, in 1854, did establish an independent Jewish Theological Seminary at Breslau. Its curriculum became a model for similar Jewish institutions within Germany, as well as elsewhere in western Europe, and the United States.

The Science of Judaism thus became an international movement. Even before disaster overtook its mother country, the Jewish Theological Seminary of America (founded in 1886) and the Hebrew University of Jerusalem (established in 1925) had inherited its standards and aims. It was in the latter two centers that the Ashkenazim were to further the tradition of scholarship which had first been established in medieval Germany.

3.   SPIRITUAL CHALLENGE AND RELIGIOUS THOUGHT

German Jewry's faith in the ways of the Lord was never allowed to remain static. It was intermittently subjected to the trials of persecution, the temptations of assimilation, and the terror of destruction. Some of the community sought escape from this situation in apostasy; but others attempted to come to terms with their historical circumstances through a unique interpretation of Judaism itself. It is these efforts, and their wider effects, which must now become the subject of our attention.

Piety

A small group of 12th and 13th century pietists known as the Hasidei Ashkenaz ("Pious of Germany") were amongst the first German Jews to re-examine their faith. For some time they were also the only ones to do so in any systematic form. In general, medieval German Jews (unlike their brethren in Spain and Islamic lands) did not indulge in theological speculation. Very often, their precarious and itinerant existence forced them to

Ḥasidei Ashkenaz

42

follow the strong practical example of the Talmud. They would, therefore, probably have sympathized with the order of our chapters, in which a survey of Jewish scholarship in Germany precedes a discussion of religious thought there. Nevertheless, the Ḥasidei Ashkenaz concentrated in the Rhenish cities, did briefly exert a wide influence which belied their small numerical strength. The reason lay as much in the problems which they tackled, as in the solutions which they proposed. For their spiritual thinking related directly to the persecutions of the Crusades and to the accompanying phenomenon of mass Jewish martyrdom.

Their theology, which stressed the unity and incorporeality *The Sources* of God and the harmony of the whole universe, was derived from various sources. Much of it came from the body of esoteric lore which the Kalonymus family (the movement's main leaders) received through a long chain of verbal tradition from Italy. They also made extensive use of such jewish mystical literature as they could obtain from Spain and Islamic lands. But simultaneously, they imbibed the superstitions of their gentile surroundings. The literature of the group contains a large body of demonological, magical, and occult elements which they could have culled only from local Christian elements. They believed that the dead stalk the synagogues, that demons and spirits encompass men from all sides, and that their leaders possessed magical powers. In consequence, the characters of such personalities as Samuel ben Kalonymus he-Ḥasid (11th century), his son Judah he-Ḥasid (c. 1150-1217), and Eliezer ben Judah of Worms (c. 1165-1230), have tended to disappear behind the many legends which grew up around them.

This strikingly large body of esoteric literature was inter- *Sefer Ḥasidim* spersed with more recognizably Jewish ethical works. One of the Ḥasidei Ashkenaz's main responses to contemporary problems was to set up a definite human ideal, a type of man and way of life to be followed. The *Sefer Ḥasidim* ("Book of the Pious"),

43

much of which was written by Judah he-Ḥasid, was both the most important and the most influential of the works which attempted to do so. Its detailed list of instructions to the pious man embraces every minute of his existence, every action of his life, and every facet of human relations. Thus it teaches the wealthy man the importance of giving charity to the poor, for unless he does so he is considered to have stolen from them. It teaches the sinner the true manner of repentance, and the piety of immersion in a frozen river in winter and of exposure to the heat during the summer. It warns the tax-payer that false declarations, although protected by such legal fictions as sleeping partnerships, bring spiritual destruction upon them and the whole community. Throughout, it is characterized by a strict and uncompromising adherence to the entire body of religious ethics.

The Ḥasidei Ashkenaz were not content with preaching to the masses. Their main purpose was to set an example which the

Title page of *Sefer Hasidim,* printed in Sulzbach, Austria, 1685. The costs of printing the book were defrayed by one Aaron ben Lipmann of Vienna.

latter would appreciate, even if they could not emulate. In an ambivalent attitude common to many self-conscious minorities, they referred to the community leadership, which they criticized, as *ra'im* (evil ones) and to the masses as *peshutim* (simple ones). They themselves, however, were *tovim* (good), *zaddikim* (righteous), or *hasidim*. Moreover, although in their outward behavior the group submitted to the full rigors of the established law, at bottom they denied its absolute validity for themselves. Thus, they distinguished between the Law of the Torah (to which the *peshutim* adhered) and the Law of Heaven (to which the *hasid* aspired). Often, the latter was the more demanding; as when ordering a thief to pay damages to his victim and not merely return him the stolen article, as prescribed by the Torah. Sometimes, however, it could be more radical; as when permitting the testimony of "honest" women, which the Torah proscribes.

Throughout, the Hasidei Ashkenaz stressed the virtues of *The Hasid* piety, in addition to learning. It was devotion which distinguished the *hasid*. He achieved proximity to God more through love, which he often found impossible to describe other than in explicit sexual symbols, than through obedience. His prayers were not formal recitals, but expressions of true inner feeling, and might therefore be said in the vernacular. He appreciated the mystical importance of the melodies to which they were chanted and of the numerical value of each letter which they contained. Humility, the quality personified by Judah he-Hasid, was the highest virtue and penitence (yet another Christian element) an exalted practice. Above all, martyrdom *(Kiddush ha-Shem)* is the supreme manifestation of love for God. Self-sacrifice, the scourge of the period, thus became a glory for which the *hasid* yearned; not as an escape from this world, but as an expression of his longing for the next.

The influence exerted by the example and teaching of the Hasidei Ashkenaz extended, even in their own day, to France and

Spain. Although many of their principles were never completely translated into practice, and sometimes aroused opposition, this small group became intimately connected with much of Jewish life. Their teachings affected many conceptions of Jewish law and some of their prayers were incorporated into the liturgy. They gave German Jewry, in particular, much of the inner strength which enabled it to survive later storms of persecution and they passed on to 18th century Polish and Russian Hasidism many of its basic precepts.

The Haskalah

The German setting of Hasidut Ashkenaz was an isolated phenomenon. Later major movements in Jewish mysticism, Messianism, and pietism emanated, not from Germany, but from Palestine (the Kabbalah), Eastern Europe and the Mediterranean (Shabbateanism), and Poland and Russia (Hasidism). Nevertheless, the Hasidei Ashkenaz did bequeath one significant facet to later German Jews. Their assimilation of certain elements of the local culture of their time was to be echoed, in the 18th century, when German Jewry made a much greater effort to come to terms with the Enlightenment, the dominant European philosophy of the age. Rationalism, the principal feature of enlightened thought, was thus of dual importance. First, as we have seen, it influenced some Germans to regard Jews as acceptable social beings. Simultaneously, it also encouraged some Jews to regard European civilization as an acceptable cultural standard. It was the aim of the Haskalah (Enlightenment) movement to provide a symbiosis between these two trends and to achieve a synthesis of modern rationalism with traditional Judaism.

Secular studies were not unprecedented amongst Jews. The Golden Age of Spanish (11th-12th century) and Italian (16th century) Jewry amply demonstrates that. Even in Germany, some Jews had departed from the traditional educational patterns as early as 1700. The circle of privileged Jews had their own incen-

Moses Mendelssohn; a portrait of 1787, the year after his death (left). Jonathan Eybeschuetz (right).

tive for doing so, but similar trends were discernible elsewhere too. Jacob Emden and Jonathan Eybeschuetz, two great 18th century German rabbis whom we shall meet again, were familiar with currents of European thought which could have reached them only through contact with non-Jewish sources, and they even made use of this knowledge in their talmudic dissertations. But neither the Orthodox rabbi nor the assimilated privileged Jew were true precursors of the Haskalah. Neither had actively attempted to accommodate the Enlightenment with Judaism. The rabbi found this unthinkable; he merely neutralized the new elements by integrating them into a traditional context. The assimilationist found it unnecessary; he simply changed his faith. Not until Moses Mendelssohn (1729-1786) burst upon Jewish history, was the attempt to be made.

Mendelssohn's biography itself illustrates his attempt to bridge two worlds. He was born into the Dessau ghetto, but before he died had won the accolades of the Berlin salons. His early education was largely (albeit not exclusively) rabbinical,

Title page of the statute book of a study group in Bamberg, 1778.

but the later writings of the "Jewish Socrates," as he was called, concerned European philosophy and German literature too. He grew up speaking Yiddish, but eventually became a master of German style. All this was accomplished, moreover, without the advantages of either inherited wealth or a prepossessing appearance (he suffered from a permanent spinal curvature) and without compromising traditional Jewish practice. Mendelssohn did raise rabbinic eyebrows when describing Judaism as "revealed legislation" rather than "revealed religion." He also aroused Orthodox opposition when he proposed that burial be deferred for three days as the secular authorities required, rather than take place immediately as Jewish law ordained. But he twice rejected the invitation of a Swiss clergyman, John Lavater, to convert. Instead, and especially in his later years, he actively denounced discrimination against Jews and in his writings (particularly *Jerusalem*) persistently defended the tenets of the Jewish faith on a rational basis.

Considerable as Mendelssohn's contributions to secular culture were, they pale in importance beside his efforts to introduce the Jewish people to that sphere. He attracted a group of disciples (called the *maskilim*), together with whom he launched a program designed to re-educate German Jewry. The traditional supremacy of the Talmud was to be challenged together with the Yiddish jargon in which it was taught. Both were to be replaced by more enlightened disciplines. A start was made with a meticulous translation of the Pentateuch into German (in Hebrew letters). Such was the magnitude of the undertaking that it took Mendelssohn and his colleague, Naphtali Herz Wessely (1725-1805), five years to complete. Such was its success that men asked whether the product was to be read for its content or for its style. Hebrew, too, was a national treasure which Mendelssohn and his band insisted on reviving. Their German Pentateuch was accompanied by a collaborative commentary in pure Hebrew, and in 1783 the *maskilim* began producing a Hebrew journal, *Ha-Me'assef*. Finally, sharing the rationalist belief in the boundless efficacy of a rational education, the *maskilim* also turned to pedagogy as a means of re-shaping Jewish life. Starting in 1778 with a Free School in Berlin, they established a series of institutions for boys and girls in which the curriculum included languages, science, history, and art. Jewish studies were to begin with a thorough grounding in grammar and the Bible, rather than

Maskilim

the Talmud. Moreover, emphasis was to be placed on training pupils for "productive" manual labor, rather than traditionally Jewish "mercantile" activity.

But Mendelssohn's German disciples were unable to preserve *The Delicate Balance* their master's delicate balance between old and new. Ultimately, they inherited more of his spirit of compromise with rationalism than of his loyalty to Judaism. Increasingly, as they followed Mendelssohn and immersed themselves in Germany's rich and attractive culture, they felt compelled to abandon the ancestral precepts which he had maintained. The ideology of the Haskalah did not thereby disappear. Indeed, it was revived in even greater strength in Eastern Europe toward the end of the 19th century. But in Germany it became little more than a prelude to apostasy. Shortly after Mendelssohn's death *Ha-Me'assef* ceased to appear, the schools abandoned their religious content, and many of his followers went over to the dominant religion, as he had gone over to the dominant culture. Among them were Mendelssohn's own children. His daughter Dorothea became the mistress, later wife, of Friedrich von Schlegel; his grandson Felix, baptized in infancy, used his genius to enrich the music of the church.

A portrait of the composer Felix Mendelssohn Bartholdy, the grandson of Moses Mendelssohn. He was baptized as a child and his father, Abraham, added the name Bartholdy because "a Christian Mendelssohn is an impossibility."

50

Solomon Maimon. He adopted the name Maimon in honor of Maimonides.

Others were unable to find peace anywhere. Solomon Maimon (c. 1753-1800), a prodigy of talmudic learning, abandoned his rabbinic career (together with his wife and child) when leaving his Polish town to pursue secular studies in Germany. But there he was shunned by the Jewish communities who were shocked by his libertine ways, and rejected by the Christian church which was frightened by his freethinking questions. Ultimately Maimon, one of the few of Kant's critics who actually understood what the latter was saying, did attain intellectual renown. Yet he remained an intellectual vagabond, always conscious of his own rootlessness. He was also a testimony to the devastating effects of Mendelssohn's ideology on a mind less stable, and more brilliant, than his own.

Solomon Maimon

Changes in Traditional Patterns
Mendelssohn's movement, like Ḥasidut Ashkenaz, had been led from above. In both cases, the bulk of German Jewry was exhort-

ed to follow, or at least idealize, the example of the initiated pioneers. With the failure of the *maskilim* to provide such leadership, the initiative passed to the body of the community. The problem remained the same, how to be both "a man in the street and a Jew at home." But it was couched in different terms. For by the early 19th century, secular culture was no longer strange to much of German Jewry. On the contrary, the problem lay in appreciating traditional Jewish practice. Many German Jews, although unwilling to join the church, nevertheless admired its stately order. In comparison, the noisy, informal, and often incomprehensible Jewish prayers appeared indecorous and unaesthetic. Increasingly, they demanded an abbreviated liturgy, prayers in the vernacular, and the introduction of an organ.

This was a movement of laymen, working without rabbinical *Reform* leadership. The first Reform service, at Sessen in 1810, was conducted by Israel Jacobson (1768-1828), financial agent to Jerome Bonaparte, King of Westphalia. The first organized "Temple," at Hamburg, was founded in 1818 by the headmaster of the Jewish school there. These men did not intend to form a new Jewish sect. Their only change in dogma (admittedly a highly significant one) was the abandonment of the traditional longing for a return to Zion. To those who regarded — as they claimed — Stuttgart as their Jerusalem, all such references to separatist aspirations were superfluous. They were therefore exorcised from the prayer book.

By the 1840s these tendencies had received an ideological justification. A new generation of university trained rabbis transformed Reform from a movement for superficial liturgical alterations into one of fundamental doctrinal changes. The Science of Judaism had already taught these men that Jewish practices were often evolutionary developments. They were therefore determined to find a form of religion and worship suitable to their own times. Thus, they discarded the old ceremonial and repudiated much of the rabbinical structure. The Bible alone was taken as authoritative. For the messianic idea of the return to Zion they substituted a concept of the "Mission of Israel," which could be accomplished only in the Diaspora. Jewry, they stressed, was solely a religious community. It existed, not in order to worship the Lord in accordance with rabbinical prescription, but to spread rational faith in the One God and His moral law.

Abraham Geiger, a leader of Reform Judaism and scholar of Wissenschaft des Judentums (left). Samuel Holdheim, one of the more radical Reform rabbis. After his death his opponents tried to prevent his burial in the section reserved for rabbis (right).

These were not views about which German Jewry was unanimous. The leaders of the Reform movement themselves varied in their degree of attachment to tradition. Their outstanding personality was Abraham Geiger (1810-1874), a native of Frankfort, a graduate of Heidelberg and Bonn, a rabbi, and a distinguished contributor to the Science of Judaism. He was radically opposed

Abraham
Geiger

53

to Orthodoxy, which he regarded as ossified by nomism and incapable of satisfying the cultured man. But Geiger, despite his romantic appearance, was not a revolutionary. He did wish to construct a new form of Judaism; but only by using materials to be found in the historical and halakhic traditions of the past. His approach was far less radical, therefore, than that of his Berlin colleague, Samuel Holdheim (1806-1860). The latter not only *Samuel* preached that Judaism was a religious domination rather than a *Holdheim* national religion (with which Geiger broadly agreed), he also did so in a synagogue in which the Sabbath was transferred to Sunday, in which congregants went bareheaded, and in which all the services were in the vernacular. These were practices which found more support amongst the later Reform congregations of America than they did in contemporary Germany. In the latter country it was caustically remarked that "there is nothing Jewish in Holdheim's sermons, except their German idiom."

But even Geiger's views proved too extreme for Zacharias *Zacharias* Frankel (1801-1875), the chief rabbi of Saxony. The only *Frankel* changes which he would permit in the traditional ritual were those which did not conflict with the spirit of historical Judaism. Thus although for a time Frankel unequivocally associated with the Reformers, he was unable to remain within their movement. Indeed, at the rabbinical conference summoned to Frankfort in 1845 to clarify Reform views on matters of theology and ritual, Frankel seceded. The issue which caused the breach was comparatively minor; he opposed abandoning Hebrew as the language of prayer. But the rift was a deep one, and reflected two contrasting views of the situation in which German Jewry found itself. Geiger was prepared to dispense with Hebrew because its survival would be an unwelcome sign that the Jews formed a "separate nationalism." Frankel, on the other hand, was not prepared to sacrifice a single element of the historical religion "for the sake of emancipation." For him, Hebrew was one expression of the genius of Judaism, which was itself the unique historical product of the Jewish mind and soul. Tradition, therefore, had to be preserved, not because it was divinely inspired, but because it was an expression of historical continuity. Frankel's "historical school," in its American version, was to be known as Conservative Judaism.

The evolution of the Reform and historical schools naturally drove the traditionalist Jews in Germany to reconsider their own position. Some felt that Orthodoxy, too, demanded a rationale. The man who attempted to supply that need was the extremely eloquent rabbi of the Adass Jeshurun congregation in Frankfort, Samson (ben) Raphael Hirsch (1808-1888). Unlike Geiger and Frankel, Hirsch believed absolutely that the Bible is the literal word of God. Unlike the traditionalists, however, he was not averse to following the Reformers in accepting the need for certain changes in the external forms of Judaism. He, too, preached in German and allowed the introduction of a choir into the services. Moreover Hirsch, who had spent a year at the University of Bonn, also acknowledged certain values in secular culture. The result was a conception of Neo-Orthodoxy: an attempted combination, within the framework allowed by rabbinic precepts, of *Torah* (the traditional law) and *derekh erez* (literally "etiquette"; here meaning secular culture). *Samson Raphael Hirsch*

This was an idea which Hirsch fully articulated in his *19 Letters* (1836; English edition, 1960) and in his later companion work *Choreb* (1837; English edition, 1962). Whilst the former consists of an imaginary correspondence between Benjamin, a "perplexed" young Jewish intellectual, and Naphtali, his traditionalist mentor, the latter contains a forceful exposition of Israel's "duties" in the Diaspora. Hirsch elaborated this theme in a highly personal translation of the Pentateuch and commentary (English edition, 1956-62), and taught the concept to a whole generation throughout the 37 years he was at Frankfort. Whilst recognizing the need for effecting a revision of externals within Judaism, he rejected changes affecting the Orthodox principles of

55

the Jewish faith. He preached that the Jews, rather than Judaism, were in need of reform; and this was an aim which he tried to realize through the three schools which he established in Frankfort, and through the periodical *Jeschurun* which he edited there. His colleague in Berlin, Azriel Hildesheimer (1820-1889), took this work a stage further when he founded the Orthodox Rabbinical Seminary there in 1873. This institution finally broke the monopoly in "scientific" Jewish studies thitherto held by Reform, and prepared future generations of Neo-Orthodox leaders and guides.

Despite the erudition with which these contending factions expounded their beliefs, their disputes were by no means conducted in a manner of quiet academic enquiry. Indeed, it is the passion of the religious controversies waged amongst German

The Disputes

Samson Raphael Hirsch, the outstanding leader of German Neo-Orthodoxy (left). Title page of Hirsch's *Jeschurun,* an Orthodox monthly. Hirsch's famous polemic against Frankel and Graetz first appeared in this journal (right).

"The Spinners," an oil painting by the German
Jewish artist Max Lieberman (1847-1935).

Heinrich Heine, a portrait by Jules Gìère, 1838.

Jewry during the mid-19th century which is often their most marked feature. As early as the Mendelssohnian era, Ezekiel Landau (1713-1793), one of the greatest rabbinic scholars in Bohemia, had referred to the *maskilim* as "a rabble of unclean birds," and proclaimed a ban on the reading of Mendelssohn's translation of the Pentateuch. Some years later, in 1819, 40 other Orthodox rabbis launched an even more strident broadside against the introduction of the organ in the Hamburg synagogue. In their collective work, *Elleh Divrei ha-Berit* ("These are the Words of the Covenant"), they threatened the "destroyers" with denunciation to the government on the grounds that religious heresy and political treason were two sides of the same coin. They also interspersed their learned quotations from the sacred texts with a choice selection of more earthy epithets: "villains, scoundrels, urchins, ignoramuses."

Neither were such comments restricted to the printed word. The religious controversy produced an equally forceful barrage of verbal complaints and communal strife. Thus Geiger's appointment as assistant rabbi at Breslau in 1838 produced a storm of protest (led by the Orthodox senior rabbi, Solomon Tiktin; 1791—1843), which lasted for two years. His appointment to a rabbinical post at Berlin in 1869 produced an equally strident outcry. Even amongst themselves, the traditionalists were dissonant. Thus they criticized Hirsch for wearing a canonical robe *Neo-Orthodoxy* during services, and it was they who first described his ideas with the pejorative term, "Neo-Orthodoxy." Hirsch himself was no more complimentary when criticizing Marcus Horovitz (1844-1910), the Orthodox rabbi who accepted the rabbinate of the general congregation at Frankfort, and refused to join Hirsch's secessionist community.

For ultimately the ideological rift had produced an institutional schism. The Neo-Orthodox were particularly unwilling to retain organizational ties with the Reformers. The possibility of co-operation was minimal; the danger of contamination was too

57

great. Hirsch, especially, preferred to set up secessionist communities. Until 1876, the difficulties of doing so were complicated by the Prussian law of 1847, which decreed that all Jews had to affiliate, and to pay taxes, to one unified Jewish community. Under these circumstances, not only were Orthodox members in practice forced to subsidize the institutions of the more numerous Reformers. They were also burdened with the additional costs of maintaining their own separate congregation, where these were formed.

The seal of the Jewish community of Augsburg, 1298.

But 1876 was the year of the *Austrittsgesetz,* a statute *The Austrittsgeset.* framed by Bismarck during his struggle against the Catholic church which included a clause (inserted at the suggestion of Hirsch) permitting Jews to leave their local community for reasons of conscience. For the individual assimilationist, desirous of becoming "undenominational," this was a golden opportunity. He could deny Judaism without having to undergo conversion to Christianity. It was no less welcome to the Orthodox communities. They could now combine undisturbed religious practice with a considerable financial saving. Consequently, several *Austrittsgemeinde* (separatist communities) sprang up in a movement which spread from Frankfort to other German cities. German Jewry was thus, for the first time, split into two organized camps.

The Return to Authenticity

The Reform, Historical, and Neo-Orthodox schools of the 19th century all attempted to furnish a philosophy of Judaism in accordance with the realities of contemporary Jewish life in Germany. In doing so, each group transformed (albeit in varying degrees) the traditional outlook which had characterized the community 200 years earlier. In the 20th century, however, Jewish philosophy in Germany took a completely different course. In attempting to come to terms, not merely with social changes but with the modern spirit of science and materialism too, Jewish thinkers found their main inspiration in the traditional communities of Eastern Europe.

Significantly, the three major philosophers of Judaism in 20th century Germany each arrived at their conclusions after coming into contact with a type of Jew who led a very different life from their own. The first was Hermann Cohen (1842-1918), professor of philosophy at Marburg University, who had undergone a vaguely assimilationist period during the 1880s and 1890s. A visit to Warsaw and Vilna in 1914, however, wrought a revolution in his philosophical outlook and in his attitude to Judaism. In his subsequent work *(The Religion of Reason from the Sources of Judaism,* published posthumously in 1919), not only did Cohen shift from an anthropocentric to a theocentric system, in which reality is rooted in God rather than human reason, he also vigorously affirmed that it was only the traditional Jew, as found in Eastern Europe, who could be said to be fulfilling the Jewish ideal. It was he who, by accepting the ancient "yoke of the commandments" was also capable of inheriting the future "yoke of the kingdom of God" — the era of true justice and peace. *Hermann Cohen*

The theology of Franz Rosenzweig (1886-1929) was influenced by a similar process. His attachment to Judaism, hitherto little more than nominal, was confirmed when he attended a Day of Atonement service in a small, Orthodox, Berlin synagogue in *Franz Rosenzwieg*

59

1913. Profoundly moved by the experience, he discarded the idea of converting to Christianity, and resolved to learn far more about Judaism. The outbreak of the first world war interrupted his efforts to do so by formal study and correspondence. But it also gave Rosenzweig, as a German soldier on the eastern front, an opportunity to observe at first hand the life of the Eastern European Jewish masses. For him, too, the Polish Jews became the authentic representatives of his race. They were a kind of yardstick against which to measure the fragmentary existence of the Jew in the western world. Where Cohen had found in traditional Judaism a means of arriving at eternal truths, Rosenzweig saw it as a means of true personal fulfillment. It was the constant preoccupation with religious practice, to an extent found only in Eastern Europe, which for Rosenzweig transformed impersonal laws into personal commandments; and which enabled the Jew to live a meaningful and valuable existence.

Rosenzweig first developed his philosophy in *The Star of Redemption* (1921), a major work which he began to write by jotting his thoughts down on postcards while at the front and sending them home to his mother for safe-keeping. On his return to civilian life, he also threw himself into the pedagogic task of turning himself and as many of his co-religionists as he could influence into "real" Jews. To this end, he founded the "Free Jewish House of Learning" in Frankfort, an institution in which students and teachers together attempted to move from the periphery of European culture, where they found themselves, towards the center of authentic Jewish sources, where they felt they belonged. Even when progressive paralysis confined him to his bed, Rosenzweig continued to exert a profound influence on Jewish thinkers through a continuing literary output of large proportions.

Martin Buber

One of Rosenzweig's collaborators in the Free School was Martin Buber (1878-1965), the Viennese born Zionist and lecturer on the Jewish religion at Frankfort University. He, too, had

Franz Rosenzweig. Despite his comparatively short life, he has had a major impact on modern Jewish religious philosophy (above left). Hermann Cohen (above right). Martin Buber; in Israel he became a legend in his own lifetime (below).

61

encountered "authentic" Jews; in his case, the hasidic groups whom he had observed whilst staying with his grandfather in Galicia. He deeply admired the rapture with which they worshipped God and was impressed by the compunction which drove them to seek Him in the recesses of emotion rather than through the processes of reason. On the basis of what he had seen, Buber was able to develop Rosenzweig's idea of a personal religion. Much of his work was done in Jerusalem after 1938, but even before then Buber had sketched the outlines of his faith. He believed that true communication with God, as attained by the Hasidim, was not achieved by worship of an object (in his phrase, an "I — it" relationship), but through a dialogue with a living being ("I — Thou"). This was a complete break with the motives which had impelled his 19th century predecessors to change the course of Jewish history in order to enable the Jew to enter the modern world. For Buber, Jewish history, because it was composed of a series of true dialogues with God, was itself sacred. As he wrote to a Christian colleague in 1933, he could admire the "perfection" of the Worms cathedral in objective terms. But, subjectively, he felt immeasurably more himself when standing amongst "the crooked, cracked, shapeless" stones of the Jewish cemetery there.

The trends in Jewish philosophy developed by Cohen, Rosenzweig, and Buber had their German life cut short after 1933. They did not, therefore, become the basis for organized religious movements there. Nevertheless, their influence upon German Jewry was profound. Between the first world war and the rise of Hitler, German Jewry came near to a climatic cultural renaissance. Jewish learning reached a peak of popularity, adult education classes began to flourish, and Jewish art galleries and museums were widely patronized. At the very moment when many German Jews were making their last (and, as Hitler proved, futile) efforts to assimilate, many others were experiencing a major revival of interest in traditional Jewish values.

4. FROM TRADE TO PROFESSION

The Trader

The earliest German Jews were international traders. Their settle- *Routes*
ment in the country was caused, not by a hasty flight from
persecution, but by a deliberate pursuit of markets. The migration of such families as the Kalonymides from Lucca in northern
Italy to Mainz in western Germany in the 9th century reflected a
similar geographical re-alignment of the trade routes to the East
at that time. With the Mediterranean route threatened by the
rivalry of various Italian cities, the northern route through Germany became increasingly prominent. It was up the Rhine and
Danube that eastern luxuries and silks were borne, and down the
Oder that pagan European slaves were exported. Jews were
attracted to both arteries. Whilst the majority migrated to
western Germany, some (the slave traders) were to be found as
far east as Magdeburg by the 10th century.

Once arrived, they were soon accorded official protection.
Thus in Speyer their charter of privileges exempted Jewish
traders from paying the customary tolls when entering or leaving
the city; in Regensburg it specifically allowed them "to sell gold,
silver, and any other kind of metals and merchandise
... according to their ancient custom." Meir ben Baruch's
responsa reveal that in Rothenburg Jewish merchants took
advantage of similar rights to trade, not only in gold and silver,
but in salted fish, wool, skins, wines, and grain, too. In the process, some of them undertook remarkably lengthy journeys.
Pethahiah of Regensburg, a wealthy 12th century Jewish mer- *Pethahiah of*
chant who wished to combine business with piety, was one *Regensburg*
example. In 1175 he embarked on a pilgrimage to Jewish shrines
in the East, and on the way passed through Poland, Russia, the
Crimea, Armenia, Babylon, and Syria. Others went west; in
apparently such large numbers that the German Emperor Barbarossa in 1168 even found it necessary to complain of his loss of

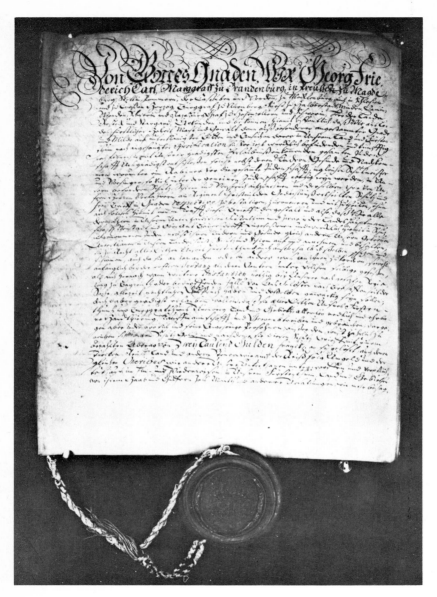

The Jews of Neustadt and Bayersdorf are offered protection by Markgraf Georg Friedrich Carl von Brandenburg, 1728.

wealthy Jewish subjects to the English King Henry II.

But by then, the German Jews had ceased to be predominantly international traders. One reason was their own reluctance to continue travelling abroad at a time when the development of busy local fairs in places like Cologne and Frankfort provided similar commercial opportunities nearer home. In fact, so marked was the tendency towards less itinerant employment that increasing numbers of Jews now turned to agriculture, viticulture, and the crafts. Those who did not take this course from choice, were often forced to do so by necessity. For the rise of Christian opposition to Jewish domination over the international trade routes had, even in the 10th century, made its influence felt. One example was provided by Pietro, Doge of Venice, a hard-headed businessman not usually given to religious contemplation. He thought it necessary to remind the Archbishop of Speyer of his Christian duty in a diplomatic note. He advised that the very least punishment which the Jews should be made to suffer for their faith was their exclusion from trading in Oriental goods.

Nearer home, the Crusades provided a more forceful reason for the gradual disappearance of the Jewish international trader in Germany. To the inherent hazards of long-distance travel, the Crusades now added the danger of officially inspired plunder and murder within the towns. To the traditional anti-Jewish bias of Christian merchants, was now added the legislation which specifically excluded Jews from the rising merchant guilds. The Jew could no longer entrust his capital to long-term trading ventures. A more prudent, and safer, course was for him to keep it in a form which could quickly be liquidated.

The Money Lender

The result was a massive switch to moneylending. This was a propitiously open field since the papal authorities, rigidly enforc- ing the biblical prohibition against usury, had in 1179 forbidden Christians to lend to each other on interest. This did not, of course, prevent all Christian commercial activity; Christian bankers merely channeled their credit into trade and industry, where it was easier to form partnerships which evaded the stigma of usury. But it did result in a scarcity of ready cash for consumer purposes; and this the Jews began to provide.

Their ability to do so was facilitated by a simultaneous modification in the Jewish attitude towards lending money to gentiles. A close reading of Deuteronomy had always revealed that interest-bearing loans were forbidden only to "your brother." Since the Jews of medieval Germany could find little evidence of a brotherly attitude towards them on the part of their Christian neighbors, no change had been necessitated in that interpretation of the text. But ancient talmudic doctrine had meanwhile prohibited any commercial dealing with gentiles "lest one learn from

A 15th century woodcut of a Jewish moneylender and his client.

Woodcut of a Jewish moneylender, Augsburg, 1531.
The borrower asks: "Please, Jew, give me cash against
a promissory note or security, and leave what is due
to you to my judgement."

their ways," and it was this restriction which the communal
rabbis of medieval Germany did show an increasing readiness to
modify. As the tosafists pointed out: "We live among the nations
and it is impossible for us to earn a living unless we deal with
them." Unless the Jew lent money to his Christian neighbor at
interest, he would have no means of paying the heavy taxes
which the latter demanded.

Through this breach poured the Jewish capital amassed
during the halcyon days of the earlier traders. About a century
after money-lending had become the main occupation of Jews in

67

England and France, those in Germany also began to provide their society with the capital which it considered disgraceful to provide, but with which it found itself unable to dispense. Articles regulating moneylending constitute the core of all charters issued to the German Jews after the 12th century. Indeed, so valuable were the taxes on Jewish moneylending, and so essential was the service itself, that several towns which expelled Jews during the 14th and 15th centuries had hurriedly to invite them back. Their cash was needed by every social class and it was put to every conceivable purpose. Extensive monastic building, lengthy judicial litigation, expensive knightly ransoms, speculative gambling ventures, costly amorous liaisons, were all financed by Jewish loans.

Jewish profits were undoubtedly commensurate with the risks involved. Rates of interest could be very high indeed; $43\frac{1}{2}\%$ was common and $86\frac{2}{3}\%$ acceptable. Although loans were dispensed on trust, most were only given on the surety of a collateral. But since redemption was often difficult, the needy Christian was thus given a new pretext for his anti-Jewish hate. Hence, many of the late medieval persecutions acquired an economic as well as a religious character. The instigators were no less anxious to destroy incriminating bonds than to eliminate accursed infidels.

Although the practice was widespread, moneylending was *Other* never the only occupation of medieval German Jews. Many *Occupations* would necessarily be subordinate agents and clerks; some would be scribes and tutors; others would be household attendants; and a large number would be students. The latter often lived in the house of their rabbinical mentor, and sometimes had no means of sustenance other than the *pletten* (meal tickets) which entitled them to call on the hospitality of other, less academic, members of the community. Religious life, indeed, itself supported a whole economic class. This included a rabbi, who became a salaried official in the 15th century; a cantor *(ḥazzan),* "the most permanent and continuous synagogue office"; a butcher, baker, and *shohet* (slaughterer), who prepared Jewish food in accordance with religious precepts; a candlemaker, book-dealer, and prayer shawl weaver; even a janitor for the ritual baths, to facilitate the conjunction of cleanliness with godliness.

Some of these individuals might even supplement their *Landowning* salaries by an income from landowning, although the difficulties of doing so within the crowded ghetto are illustrated by the following example: In the Laurenz parish of Cologne a Jewish couple in 1322 sold an eighth and one ninety-sixth portion of "a large house," in which two other co-religionists owned another quarter and one-sixteenth part. Others might turn outside the ghetto walls completely for a livelihood. One who did so with some initial success was Suesskind von Trimberg (c. 1200-1250), a minstrel and German poet who, for a time, achieved great popularity amongst the Christians.

Moreover moneylending, although distasteful, limiting, and often dangerous, itself contained the seeds of other occupations. Jewish moneylenders frequently had to repair the collateral in their hands. They also had to sell it whenever it was not redeemed. Tailoring, jewelling and second-hand trading were thus integral parts of their occupation. Increasingly during the 14th and 15th centuries, they also acted as intermediaries between the large agricultural producers (such as the local manor in the district to which they had been scattered), and the rising city merchants. Eventually, they also came to control the major part of the trade across the Polish-German border. From there it was but a short step to resuming, in the 16th century, their wider financial contacts with co-religionists in the Netherlands, France, and the Ottoman Empire.

The Court Jew
The commercial expertise and international contacts with the Jews thus acquired would have been appreciated by most rulers.

The mercantilist, ambitious, and absolutist German princes of the 17th and 18th centuries found such talents invaluable. To them the Jew with capital and experience was a distinct commercial proposition; an asset worth preserving if at hand and worth acquiring if not. Thus it was that, during the 17th and 18th centuries, Jews were often asked to re-settle in parts of Germany from which they had been ignominiously banished a few centuries earlier. They were invited to Leipzig in order to revive the trade fair; to Brandenburg in order to stimulate industry; and to Hamburg in order to promote commerce, a task which Sephardi refugee bankers from Portugal accomplished with distinction. Even then the story was not complete. The absolutist princes did not merely seek merchants and traders. They also sought private state servants, men who owed loyalty to no rival state or corporation, and whose demands for rewards could not be too high. Such men they found, and created, in the Court (or privileged) Jew.

The medieval Jewish moneylender and the later Court Jew *Function* differed in both function and character. The former's service to his prince had been limited to the supply of cash; their relationship was circumscribed by the fact that he performed the same function for other people. The Court Jew was more restricted in his employers, and yet more diverse in his employments. Admittedly, he followed traditional practice when providing the prince's treasury with a ready fund of credit. But he was also expected to use his initiative and international connections to ensure that the army, the most important instrument of the prince's power, had a regular flow of supplies, too. "In this way the banker and financial agent became the army contractor, the Court purveyor, and the commercial entrepreneur ... He was used in secret missions, political councils, armistice negotiations, and military operations." By the middle of the 17th century, he had become an essential functionary in almost every German principality. Court Jews served enlightened atheists, orthodox

70

Calvinists, Lutheran Protestants, and fanatic Catholics. They were to be found in the south and in the north, at the courts of warlike prelates and frivolous princes, in areas where Jewish communities had long been in existence and in places where they were yet to be founded.

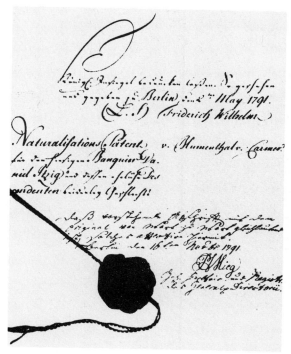

Naturalisations Patent, the document conferring full Prussian citizenship on Daniel Itzig and his descendants. It was given to him on May 2, 1791.

The history of German Jewry during the absolutist age is *Daniel Itzig* studded with these personalities. Many of them began their careers as dealers in precious stones, a commodity whose perennial value was especially marked at a time when debasements of the coinage were regular occurences. This was a situation which Daniel Itzig (1723-1799), the son of a horse dealer who became the first Jew to receive full Prussian citizenship (1791), exploited to the full. Even in his case, however, the mere possession of

Samson Wertheimer (1658-1724), court Jew of Emperors Leopold I, Joseph I and Charles VI. He also served as rabbi in Vienna (left). Joseph Suess Oppenheimer in the cage in which his body was exhibited after his execution. Artist unknown, 1723 (right).

valuables was no guarantee of service. The Court Jew also had to be ambitious, resourceful, and very often reckless too. Above all, he had to be adaptable to the needs of his employer. This last quality was symbolized by the Gomperz family, who served as

Court purveyors to six successive rulers in Berlin. To Frederick I (1657-1713), the luxury-loving first king of Prussia, they furnished jewels; to his more military-minded son, Frederick William I (1688-1740), they supplied "tall fellows for his guard."

Most Court Jews benefited financially from their positions. Only such spendthrifts as Leffman Behrends (1643-1714), financier to the elector of Hanover, would come close to bankruptcy. Most could also look forward to social advantages. As privileged Jews they would never have to be confined to the ghetto. Yet, for that very reason, the Court Jew trod a lonely path. Whilst his religion and descent continued to distinguish him as an outsider at court, his elevated position and function also isolated him from his fellow Jews. Moreover, proximity to the throne could be dangerous too. Nothing, it is said, succeeds like success. In the world of the Court Jew, nothing could succeed but success. His position, his very life, depended upon his usefulness to his absolutist ruler; and whilst ability could raise him very high, an unkind turn of fate could bring him equally low. In his short career, *Joseph* Joseph Suesskind Oppenheimer (*Jud Suess;* 1698/9-1738) the *Oppenheimer* subject of the novel *Power* (1927) by L. Feuchtwanger, experienced both extremes. Suave, good looking, and related to Jewish financiers throughout Germany, he was appointed state counsellor to the Duke of Wuerttemberg in 1733. In this position he lived in luxurious splendor and wielded supreme power over nobility, clergy, and populace alike. In the course of his duties he trampelled on privileged orders and propelled the state under his charge into the modern world of ruthless centralization. But Oppenheimer, who controlled so much, ultimately possessed very little. On March 19, 1737, the Duke of Wuerttemberg suddenly died; on the same day Oppenheimer was himself arrested and charged with treason. Notwithstanding an inadequate trial, on April 2, 1738, he was hanged. His remains were then exhibited in an iron cage, a public symbol of the precarious isolation in which all Court Jews lived.

The Man of Business and Finance

For all their prominence, the Court Jews were by their nature exceptions. The majority of German Jewry during the absolutist age still earned a far more prosaic living, as retail pedlars, old clothes dealers, and middlemen. Their situation changed only with the industrialization of Germany in the 19th century. This process, rightly termed a "revolution," did not merely produce more tools, more clothes, and more commodities by using new means of power and new machines. It also produced them at a pace and with a regularity which demanded equally novel methods of supply, management, and distribution. These were the fields which German Jews now entered.

In so doing, they did not break completely with traditional patterns. Admittedly, they benefited more than most groups from the loosening of the restrictions on their place of habitat and work. The number of German Jews engaged in manual labor, therefore, dwindled to insignificant proportions. But it was not the Jews, for instance, who pioneered the heavy industries of the Ruhr. Emil Rathenau (1838-1915), the founder of the giant electric corporation AEG, typified an exception rather than the rule. In general, German Jews merely refined their former activities. Previously, they had been middlemen between town and country; now they specialized as entrepreneurs in the larger wool, grain, fur, and metal trades. Previously they had dealt in old clothes; now they became the dominating influence in the clothing, textile, and hat industries. Thus, by the end of the 19th century about half of the manufacturing firms in the clothing industry were owned by Jews and one of them, Gebrueder Simon, became under James Simon's (1851-1932) management, one of the largest in the world. Previously, Jews had been petit bourgeois retailers; now they became pioneers of department stores. Of the five German chain stores in the 1930s — Schocken, Tietz, Wertheim, Karstadt, and Kaufhof — Jews owned three and managed the other two. Even the ancient tradi-

The Industrial Revolution

74

Mayer Amschel Rothschild, the founder of the dynasty (above left). Postage stamp issued in West Germany in 1957 commemorating the centenary of the birth of Albert Ballin, the German shipping magnate. He was a close adviser of Kaiser William II and in 1918 was entrusted with the armistice negotiations (above right). The Schocken department store in Chemnitz. It was designed by Eric Mendelsohn in 1928/ 1929 (below).

tion of international trading found its modern echo in the activities of Albert Ballin (1857-1918), the shipping magnate and owner of the HAPAG line, the only member of his Kaiser's circle to remain unbaptized.

It was in the sphere of finance that the essentially Jewish *Rothschilds* combination of continuity and ingenuity was to reach its apogee in modern Germany. The mere mention of the name of Rothschild sufficiently illustrates the point. The family did not have a long financial tradition. As recently as the 17th century they were moderate Frankfort merchants. Even the first banker of the name Mayer Amschel (1744-1812) owed his major breakthrough to a fortuitous coincidence. It was not as a financier, but as a collector of old coins that he came to the attention of William, future elector of Hesse-Cassel. The fact that the latter, besides being a passionate numismatist, was also heir to the largest private fortune in Europe, was even more providential. But Mayer exploited his opportunity brilliantly. When Napoleon's soldiers swept into Frankfort, he managed to keep William's wealth in safe-keeping in the catacombs of the Jewish quarter. He then used those resources as a basis for investment elsewhere. The prudent and discreet manner in which this was done in London by Mayer's son, both increased William's fortune and made the Rothschild name. Four of Mayer's sons established branches of the parent bank in Paris, London, Naples, and Vienna. Mayer and his first-born Amschel Mayer (1773-1855) continued to operate from Frankfort, where they ramified their commercial interests and increased the Rothschild fortune and fame. Less than a century after old Mayer Amschel's momentous meeting with his ruler, his grand-nephew, Mayer Karl (1820-1886), had become the first Jew ever to be appointed to the Prussian House of Lords.

And yet the Rothschilds were only one star, albeit the brightest, in a whole galaxy of German-Jewish finance. Even in Frankfort itself there was Samuel von Haber (1764-1839), who in 1853 converted the inherited wealth of generations into the founding capital of the mighty Darmstaedter Bank. In Berlin there was Gerson von Bleichroeder (1822-1839), the son of a Rothschild employee, who became personal financial agent to the great Bismarck himself. In Cologne there was Abraham Oppenheim (1804-1878), one of the most influential bankers in the Rhineland. And behind even these, there was a complete sub-category of lesser figures. One example was provided by the Jewish stockbrokers, whose domination of the Berlin exchange in the 19th century was so pronounced that the statutes of that institution found it necessary to lay down that two of the four directors must be Christians. Moreover, when Jewish participation in stockbroking declined (to only 3.8% in 1925), a generation of joint stock bankers rose to take its place. In 1933 Jews still carried a leading voice in the management of the Dresdner and Deutsche Banks, which earlier Jews had helped to found.

Men of Science and Letters

For the German Jew, emancipation meant more than the freedom to pursue his trade unhindered by legal restrictions. It also meant the freedom to escape from it. The centers of German arts and science, which had once opened their doors only to the privileged few, suddenly found their auditoriums filled with the many Jews eager to study and teach there. A large proportion of these came from Eastern Europe, where increasing numbers of Russian-Jewish *maskilim* found that they had few opportunities of obtaining a university education. Thus it was that in 1892 Chaim Weizmann (1874-1952), the future first president of Israel and a native of the Russian Pale of Settlement, first arrived in Darmstadt. But the vast majority of the Jews attending German universities came from Germany itself. Under their influence, the old community of traders, moneylenders, and petty businessmen became almost unrecognizable. Around the mid-19th century the tradition of Jewish scholarship, which had hitherto benefited only Jewish culture, began to enrich the life of non-Jewish Germany too. Thereafter, increasing numbers of Jewish physicians examined Christian patients, Jewish advocates defended Christian clients, Jewish artists played to Christian audiences, and Jewish teachers even taught Christian schoolchildren the rudiments of their own language.

There was virtually no field of intellectual activity in Germany during the period 1850-1930 in which the Jews did not play a commanding, at times even a dominating, role. In some cases, their accomplishments can be regarded as particularly successful links in a long chain of Jewish tradition. Thus, the ancient Jewish stress on the value of life, and on the need to preserve it, was reflected in the high proportion (15.5% in 1924) of Jewish doctors in Germany. Their long legal tradition found a similar echo in the numerous Jewish lawyers (26% of total in 1924). The creative and artistic talents which had previously found expression in manuscript illuminations, liturgical compositions, and biblical dramatics, now became transformed into more secular fields. Kurt Weil (1900-1950), the son of a *ḥazzan,* became one of Germany's most prominent composers and Max Reinhardt (1873-1943), an emigree from Vienna, the most powerful influence on its drama. These figures were only the most prominent representatives of a wider Jewish passion for the stage. No wonder, therefore, that the German theater was one of the first victims of Hitler's anti-Semitic policy. As early as April 10, 1933, one English newspaper correspondent noted: "The theaters are beginning to suffer from the impoverishment of the Jews, who have always been lavish patrons."

The prominence of those who refined traditional Jewish tastes was exceeded by the greatness of those who became pioneers in new fields of Jewish cultural interest. Thus the German dye industry owed much of its success to the Jewish organic chemist and Nobel laureate, Richard Willstaeter (1872-1942); and the German press owed much of its reputation to the *Frank-*

furter Zeitung, founded by Leopold Sonneman (1831-1909). Before 1939, Germany as a whole owed much of its prestige in the scientific world to the eleven Jews amongst its 38 Nobel Prize winners. These included Otto Wallach (1847-1931), the organic chemist; Fritz Haber (1868-1934), who synthesized ammonia from hydrogen and nitrogen; and the great Albert Einstein (1879-1955).

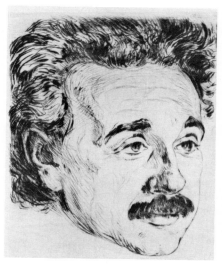

Albert Einstein, a portrait by Hermann Struck.

Not every Jewish pioneer in these fields was accorded equal fame within Germany. Some were denied recognition by the force of unfortunate circumstances. For instance David Schwarz (1845-1897), the first man to invent a dirigible airship, died of shock when told that the German government would finance his project. It was promptly bought up by the more widely known Count Zeppelin. Far more were the victims of official anti-Semitism. Willstaeter had to resign his university post in Munich as early as 1924; after the rise of Hitler such occurences became common. Even Einstein had to emigrate whilst seeing his science of nuclear physics disparaged as *judenphysik* by some Nazis.

Judenphysik

79

Such men, who had revolutionized the pattern of Jewish occupation in Germany almost as much as they had revolutionized their chosen fields of interest, could find escape only in flight to more liberal lands.

5. GOVERNMENT AND THE GOVERNED

A State Within a State

Every medieval German Jew had two masters. One was the gentile government, the other was the Jewish community. The former, especially when inspired by the Church or goaded by the mob, was generally the more oppressive. It might impose the isolation of the ghetto, the indignity of the yellow badge, and the inferior status of an "imperial servant." It could also exercise the prerogative of arbitrary taxation. Every German Jew had to pay a "coronation tax" when his ruler ascended the throne; a "penny offering" every year he sat on it; and, at various intervals, additional hefty sums to ease his stay there. Those in medieval Frankfort, for instance, were ordered to supply parchment for the royal chancellory, bedding for the court, and utensils for the kitchen.

These were the burdens incumbent on every German Jew. *Community* Yet for most of them the external government remained remote. *Rule* None except the most exceptional ever came into contact with it as an individual; the vast majority met with it only in their collective capacity as part of the community. Medieval rulers, who regulated all society into self-governing corporate groups, had bestowed autonomy on the Jews too. Their legal status was akin to that of the nobles and serfs within the feudal system, the burgesses and guilded merchants in the towns, or the clergy and religious orders within the Church. The authority of the ruler who governed each individual was expressed only through the separate legislature of every group. Thus for the individual Jew it

Major medieval Jewish communities in Germany in the 13th century.

One of the silver goblets of the Frankfort *Ḥevra Kaddisha*. The acrostic of the poem inscribed on it forms the names of some of the leading members and the medallions contain emblems of the family names. At the annual *Ḥevra Kaddisha* banquet, the goblet would be filled with rare wine and passed around among all the members. The goblet dates from the early 18th century.

was the community, not the government, which administered justice, levied taxes, and maintained the fabric of society.

It even regulated the right of local residence. As early as the 11th century, Jewish communities along the Rhine exercised their discretion when admitting co-religionists to their localities. Some newcomers had to acquire the right by purchase or hire; others could be excluded altogether *(Ḥerem ha-Yishuv)* on moral or economic grounds. Whichever the case, he whom the community might let in, the community might also cast out. In its hands, the threat of excommunication *(ḥerem)* was transformed from a forbidding spiritual safeguard into the ultimate social sanction. Since the Christian authorities consistently supported the decisions of Jewish courts in this matter, the *ḥerem* implied complete ostracism from all society. Probably for this reason, it was rarely applied.

Within the communities themselves, there was a large measure of social cohesion. The common danger of persecution was one levelling factor; the common burden of taxation was another. As early as the 11th century, community ordinances decreed that no member of the group had the right to secure an exemption from the public burden by a private deal with the authorities. Moreover, the German Jews shared essential social institutions. Their communities maintained the synagogues, schools, ritual bathhouses, abattoirs, bakeries and cemeteries. Many also administered hospitals, and some even wedding halls *(tanzhauser)*. Even the smallest possessed a charitable service *(gemilut ḥasadim)* for the poor and a burial society *(ḥevra kaddisha)* for the deceased. A range of statutes, dating mainly from the 12th and 13th centuries, further emphasized the importance of communal responsibility. Sumptuary laws, for instance, precluded conspicuous, and divisive, ostentation in dress and entertainment. Commercial regulations discouraged commercial competition; even in the overcrowded ghettos Jews were forbidden to vie with each other for the lease of a house from a gentile. If, notwithstanding, members of the community did consider themselves victims of an injustice, they were at liberty to proclaim the fact by interrupting the synagogue service *(bittul ha-tamid)*. Many did so with irreverent frequency and until 1876 the cry of *Ich klamme* ("I claim") was permitted to disturb the prayers.

Not that communal government was democratic. A wealthy minority paid most of the communal taxes (scholars, orphans, widows, paupers, and the disabled were among a host of people exempted), and they therefore occupied most of the communal offices. They invariably acted as tax-assessors, tax-collectors, synagogue wardens, and charity administrators. Elections did exist, often in a bewildering variety of methods. But the franchise was always denied to women, invariably restricted to the *meliores* ("good" persons), and sometimes, as in 14th century Worms, taken away from particular families. In these instances the minority, meaning the disenfranchised majority, was powerless. By the 13th century, Eliezer ben Joel ha-Levi had established the principle that a majority decision also obligated the opposing minority and unanimity was not required.

The Rule of the Rabbi

But in the classic medieval German community, not even the influence wielded by the wealthy could match the authority exercised by the rabbis. Lay control of the community was possible only with their co-operation and assent; decisions taken by lay members of the judiciary *(bet din)* were only effective if in accordance with their interpretation of talmudic law. In purely ritualistic matters, the authority of the rabbi was uncontested. In social honors, he was second to none. By the late 14th century, the prestige of the German rabbis had been symbolized by the title of *morenu* ("our teacher/guide") which they all bore.

Long before then, the rabbi had also become responsible for the framing of communal directives *(takkanot ha-kahal)*. Origin- *Takkanot* ally designed as guides to religious practice, these regulations quickly developed into ordinances of communal government. They thus became the means by which medieval German rabbis strengthened community life and increased communal authority. Throughout the medieval period, one class of *takkanot*, dealing with Sabbath observance and the dietary laws, are interspersed with another, forbidding Jews to apply to non-Jewish courts or to accept appointments from the gentile authorities.

The sources of rabbinic authority were varied. Initially, it *Gershom ben* derived from the respect traditionally accorded to the hallowed *Judah* combination in one man of piety and scholarship. Thus, the influence of Gershom ben Judah (c. 960-1028), one of the community's first talmudic scholars, was not restricted to the circle of his yeshivah at Mainz. His halakhic decisions were respected throughout the country and he was widely referred to as *Me'or ha-Golah* ("Light of the Exile"). Amongst the many famous *takkanot* attributed to him are the ban on polygamy *(Herem de-Rabbenu Gershom)*, and on divorcing a wife against her will. In other instances, such as the Kalonymides, similar piety and scholarship were complemented by wealth. In yet a third category, they were supported by qualities of leadership. Meir ben *Meir ben* Baruch of Rothenburg, for instance, acted for almost half a cen- *Baruch* tury as the supreme Jewish court of appeals in Germany. He

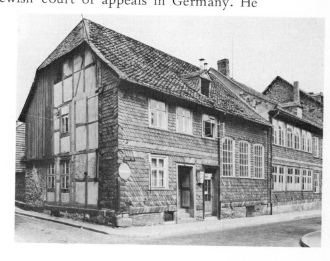

The synagogue of Goslar — now a bakery. A typical 19th century German dwelling house. The photograph was taken in 1959.

Divorce proceedings, Germany, 18th century. Top left: The divorce is written. The wife weeps; the husband speaks to the members of the court. Top right: the bill of divorcement (*get*) is examined by the rabbis. Bottom left: the husband throws the *get*. Bottom right: the wife catches it.

deliberately took it upon himself to act as arbiter between communities and their members, between settled and new settlers, and between various communities in their mutual relations. Thus, almost single-handed this lucid, terse, and occasionally abrasive scholar fashioned and formulated the laws and rituals of contemporary Ashkenazi Jewry. The manner of his death merely sym-

Fig. XVII. *Von der Begrœbuiß.* *pag. 174.*

P.IV.

Three stages of burial, Johann Bodenschatz' *Kirchliche Ver-
fassung der heutigen Juden,* Germany, 1740. Top: the body
is taken to the purification hall. Lower left: the corpse is
put into the coffin for burial. Lower right: mourners throw
grass and earth behind them as they leave the graveside.

bolized the strength of character which he had displayed
throughout his life. In 1286 he was committed to prison for
attempting to lead a widespread exodus from Germany in protest
against the special taxes imposed upon the Jews. He died there,
because he refused to allow the community to ransom him, lest
this give rise to further attempts at extortion.

Not even Meir of Rothenburg, however, can be described as an offical "chief rabbi" of all German Jewry. Unity, in this formal sense, was rejected. Ever since the Babylonian and Palestinian academies had lost their universal influence, each individual Jewish community cherished its sovereign rights and its independence from outside authority. Inter-communal synods of rabbis, on the French model, were occasionally held in Germany. The most influential and famous of these were those convened, *Shum* after 1220, by the communities of Speyer, Worms, and Mainz (collectively known as *"Shum"*). They dealt with such diverse matters as the scope of communal taxation and the levity allowed to bridegrooms. But even their decisions *(takkanot Shum)* were no more than guidelines, which individual communities implemented as they wished. Rupert of Wittelsbach did attempt to appoint one rabbi *Hochmeister* over all German Jewry in 1407. A Jew, Seligmann Oppenheim Bing aspired to the same idea in 1455. But, as in the case of Germany itself, all efforts at centralization were frustrated by the forces of particularism. They could also be discouraged by the secular government. When, in 1603, a large gathering of rabbis met at Frankfort to draft a form of national constitution for German Jewry, the government accused them of treason and imprisoned them for their pains.

The Protection of the Shtadlan

Significantly, the first acknowledged *Befehlshaber der ganzen* *Joseph of* *Judenschaft* (Commander of all [German] Jewry) was not a *Rosheim* rabbi at all, but a layman named Joseph (Joselmann) ben Gershon (c. 1478-1554) from Rosheim near Strasbourg. Neither, moreover, did his title reflect learning; for Joseph was a rather mediocre scholar. It indicated, rather, that by the 16th century German Jewry needed a figure with the ability to obtain access to the gentile authorities and to intercede with them on the community's behalf. Joseph, a ready speaker and a man of the

Havdalah spice box, silver, partly gilt, Germany, 17th century.

A *Mizraḥ* panel, used to indicate the location of east, the direction of prayer. Given as a gift to a German synagogue in 1833 on the occasion of a wedding.

A page from a *Haggadah* written in Altona - Hamburg, 1740. The *Haggadah* was written and illuminated by Joseph bar David Leipnick, a Jewish Moravian artist. The page, illustrating the labors of the Israelites in Egypt, in fact shows contemporary Jews working in a German town.

סידור

שפה ברורה

מסודר בשלימות הסידור ומדויק בתכלית הדיוק

ומתורגם אשכנזית

מאת

וואָלף ב״ר שמשון א״ש היידנהיים

רעדלהיים

שנת תקפ״ג לפ״ק

Roedelheim,

verlegt u. gedruckt in der privilegirten Buchdruckerey
von W. Heidenheim 1822.

Title page and frontispiece of Wolf Heidenheim's *siddur, Safah Berur-ah.* It was published in Roedelheim in 1822 and contains the prayers, *seliḥot,* and *piyyutim* for all occasions. The German translation of the text is in Hebrew characters. Special editions were printed for bridegrooms to give their brides; this is indicated in the plaque held by the cherubs. The picture, which is not from a Jewish source, was changed in subsequent editions; in some the scenery became more German and the cherubs were clothed. The structure in the foreground is an incense altar.

world (and the subject of a novel by M. Lehmann, written in 1925 and translated as *Tales of Yore* in 1947), was amply qualified for the task. He was also highly successful. We catch glimpses of him hovering in the background at Imperial diets, badgering German rulers for letters of protection, and speaking up for communities as far apart as his native Rosheim in Alsace and Pezinok in Hungary. His watchfulness immeasurably improved the lot of contemporary German Jewry. It also introduced a new figure into the hierarchy of Jewish communal leadership, that of the *shtadlan* (intercessor).

The novelty of this position was substantive; for although Joseph's methods were not necessarily new, the status which he and his fellow *shtadlanim* acquired was revolutionary. Acquaintance with authority now rivalled proficiency in learning as the criterion for leadership. This became particularly so in the 17th and 18th centuries, when the long list of Court Jews obtained the ear of their respective princes, and numerous Jewish communities benefited thereby. Not every Court Jew was also a *shtadlan;* hence the difference in nomenclature. Some sensed the difficulty in combining personal service for the ruler with communal service on behalf of his Jewish subjects. Neither was every *shtadlan* a rival of rabbinic authority. Many saw to it that their daughters married promising young scholars; others vied for the privilege of patronizing scholarship. Thus, in Frankfort on the Oder, Behrend Lehmann (1661-1730) financed the first printing of the Talmud in Germany (1697-1699). Not to be outdone, Samson Wertheimer (1658-1724), another Court Jew, sponsored a second edition in Frankfort on the Main (1720-1723).

But those Court Jews who did accept the additional responsibility of *shtadlanut,* also increased their own power over their Jewish fellows. In the 17th century Israel Aaron, who until the admission of Austrian refugees was the only Jew in Berlin, translated this into personal terms. He forced even the most distinguished of the Viennese emigrees to sign a legal pledge that they would not compete with him in business. Elsewhere, communal authority was the prize. In several instances, it was to the Court Jew that communities owed their very rights to legal existence, as

90

well as their freedom to worship in accordance with the manner of their choice. They, therefore, naturally cherished this personage as the "sovereign guiding father of the community" and, equally obviously, chose him as their tax-assessor, inspector, and collector. In the case of the Van Gelderns in Dusseldorf, these were positions which one family held for generations. Increasingly, therefore, the *shtadlan*-Court Jew assumed the title of "chief elder." Inexorably, his power over the community began to supersede that of the rabbi. By the 18th century, it was the *shtadlan* who called and conducted community meetings, his word which was communal law, and his the decisive voice in the election of a rabbi.

The prestige of the German rabbinate, meanwhile, suffered a severe blow. For between 1751 and 1764 two of its greatest figures were engaged in a dispute which divided and dismayed German Jewry, and which thus further weakened rabbinic authority. The cause of this upheaval, as of so many others in 18th century Jewish life everywhere, was Shabbetai Zevi (1626-1676), the Jew from Smyrna who had claimed to be the Messiah. After his apostasy (1666) the vast majority of German Jewry (who had been no less shattered by this event than their brethren elsewhere) lost all faith in him. Yet, even after his death, others secretly and illicitly remained Shabbateans. In this case, the person accused of doing so was Jonathan Eybeschuetz (1690/95-1764), rabbi of Metz and Altona — learned, obstinate, and a mystic. In 1751 he was found to have written some amulets containing supposedly Shabbatean formulas. His accuser was Jacob Emden (1697-1776), brilliant, wilful, and obstinate; a man who devoted much of his time and private printing press in Alsace to attacking the Shabbateans and who, incidentally, had been one of Eybeschuetz's competitors for the rabbinate of Altona. The details of their passionate polemic need not delay us. It was characterized, throughout, by Eybeschuetz's rather weak defense; it was complicated, in 1760, when his son proclaimed

Eybeschuetz- Emden

91

himself to be a Shabbatean prophet. For as long as it lasted the dispute caused a deep rift throughout German (and much of European) Jewry and at one point even necessitated a rather degrading appeal to the Christian authorities in Hamburg for a

Franckfurther Jud und Jüdin.

Typical Jewish costume in Frankfort, early 18th century.

judicial ruling. Ultimately, it contributed to a general, albeit often unspoken, feeling that the spiritual guidance of the rabbi contributed less to the stability of the community than did the *shtadlanut* of the Court Jew.

In the final analysis, however, power to the Court Jew was power to the ruler. At the very moment when the 18th century Enlightenment was weakening many of the religious ties within the community, the 18th century *shtadlan* was also contributing to its loss of autonomy. Originally intended as an intercessor against government discrimination, he eventually became a means of government interference in its management. Thus, in Berlin, it was the government which decided that no meeting of the community council could be held without the presence of Jost Liebman (c. 1640-1702), the local Court Jew. Elsewhere, as in the Palatinate, such meetings were also attended by government "Commissioners for Jewish Affairs." The *landjudenschaft*, self-governing communal bodies which German communities established in the 16th century in order to regulate taxation, increasingly lost their exclusiveness. Their reports were scrutinized by

Exterior view of the synagogue of Bielefeld, 1904-1938.

93

the state, not the community; their records were compiled in German, not Hebrew; and their penalties enforced by the secular courts, not the Jewish *bet din*. The Jews had lost their autonomy even before they had gained their emancipation.

Unity and Division

The German Jewish communities supervised by the *shtadlan* shared one important organizational feature with those which had formerly been ruled by the rabbi. Both had been highly particularist; unwilling, or unable, to form part of a wider national union. By the turn of the 20th century this was no longer the case. Each community did remain self-governing. In general, it had a representative council elected by the community members (including women after 1918), and an executive committee elected in turn by this body and consisting of 3 to 7 members. But the individual communities were no longer isolated and independent. Instead, the formal unity of the separate German states within one national Reich had been reflected by the formal incorporation of all German Jewry into national institutions.

Community Council

In part, of course, this was not coincidental. German Jewry could hardly fail to be affected by the factors making for general German unity. The replacement of several princes by one common emperor, and of distinguishing privileges by uniform emancipation, also encouraged the replacement of particularist communities by national institutions of Jewish government. Much of this process was also due to demographic factors. In response to the industrialization of the 19th century the German Jewish community not only grew, it also became more concentrated and more urbanized. Whereas in 1816 the vast majority of German Jews still lived in small and isolated communities, by 1916 most had settled in the large cities — Breslau, Leipzig, Cologne, Hamburg, Frankfort, and especially Berlin which eventually comprised almost one-third of the whole community.

Centralized Representation

94

These, therefore, now became natural centers of organized Jewish life.

For there can be no doubt that Jewish life in Germany continued to be highly organized. National institutions existed for every conceivable purpose. One, the *Central-Verein* (Central Organization of German Citizens of the Jewish Faith), had been founded in Berlin in 1893 in order to co-ordinate communal defense against anti-Semitism. Another, the *Hilfsverein der Deutschen Juden,* had been established in 1901 in order to combine communal efforts for the improvement of the social and political condition of Jews in Eastern Europe and the Orient. A third, the *Zentralwohlfartstelle,*was set up in 1917 as a central welfare bureau for the supervision of Jewish hospitals, clinics, and sanitoriums, and eventually had some 2,000 welfare agencies attached to it. All these had been accompanied by the national Jewish institutions for higher education and culture, and by the national networks of schools and synagogues established by the various leaders of differing religious elements. Many were supervised by regional community unions, like the *Pruessischer Landesverband Juedischer Gemeinden* (founded in 1921), which acted as a liaison between the Prussian communities and the government. All were kept in constant touch with each other by such weekly newspapers as the *Juedische Rundschau* and the *Israelitisches Familienblatt* and by such party periodicals and literary journals as *Der Israelit* (Agudat Israel) and *Der Jude* (Zionist).

Central-Verein

Not even during this period of increasing uniformity, however, could German Jewry achieve true unity. The social and cultural cohesion which had characterized the medieval community had vanished. It had been weakened by the religious differences which had led to the *Austrittsgemeinde* and by the forces of assimilation in the 19th century. It was further undermined by the subsequent waves of Jewish immigrants from the east *(Ostjuden).* The latter largely evinced a distinct reluctance to abandon their traditional Jewish manners, practices, and even

Ostjuden

dress. Their presence, therefore, offended the old German Jewish families little less than the Germans themselves. Even in many of the communities where they constituted a substantial proportion of the membership, the *Ostjuden* were denied the right to vote on communal matters or to participate in communal government. The *Deutsch-Israelitischer Gemeindebund* (DIGB) was founded for this very purpose at Leipzig in 1869, and even established its headquarters in Berlin in 1882. But it, too, eventually found itself dealing only with the more peripheral (although no less vital) field of supporting weak communities or organizing Jewish teachers' conferences. It had been defeated, not so much by particularism as by the impossibility of reconciling different factions within the community.

Zionism, the movement which demanded an independent *Zionism* Jewish existence in a separate Jewish state, divided German Jewry even further. Its proud display of Jewish nationalism was naturally offensive to those who had long denied such sentiments. Moreover, its support among the *Ostjuden* was distasteful to the more acculturated, older, segments of the community. The Zionist credo was equally decried, although for different reasons, by certain Orthodox figures. The latter found Zionism too secular and considered that the Zionists were too eager to speed the messianic process which was meant to await God's good time. German rabbis of this persuasion had made their impact felt as early as 1897. They had then publicly issued a protest against the Zionist movement (hence the sobriquet *protestrabbiner*), and had forced the organizers of the First Zionist Congress to remove its venue from Munich to Basle. By 1912 this group, together with their Hungarian and East European colleagues, had formed yet another movement, the Agudat Israel.

Not all of German Orthodoxy was anti-Zionist. The religious Mizrachi party, and its youth offshoot, Bachad, struck deep roots in Germany. Neither was all co-operation between the non-religious Zionists and the anti-Zionists impossible. The two sec-

96

tions combined in 1922, when establishing the Keren ha-Yesod and in 1929, in an enlarged Jewish Agency. Such glimpses of communal unity were just as well. For after 1933 the Jewish communities of Germany were to be tested in a way which demanded a spirit of cohesion and co-operation unprecedented even in medieval times.

View of old cemetery at Ebern, Bavaria.

6. DESTRUCTION AND DESOLATION

On January 30, 1933, the ageing president of the German Republic, Paul von Hindenberg (1847-1934), appointed Adolf Hitler (1889-1945) chancellor of the Reich. From that day, the history of German Jewry was irrevocably changed. Hereafter, in an ascending scale of unprecedented terror and unparalleled barbarity, the Jews of Germany were to lose their liberties, property, and (in many cases) their lives.

Anti-Semitism

Why was it that this Holocaust, which ultimately engulfed much of Jewry elsewhere too, should have originated in Germany? Part of the answer must be sought in the long German tradition of hatred for the Jews, to which attention has already been drawn. Friedrich Nietzsche (1844-1900), the German philosopher, probably exaggerated when stating that he had yet to meet a German who was not an anti-Semite (he is himself to be excluded from that generalization). Nevertheless, it remains true that the medieval conception of the Jews as Christ-killers, blood-suckers, and well-poisoners had never completely vanished. The blood libel, in pure medieval form, was revived at Xanten in the Rhineland in 1892 and at Hanau in Bavaria as late as 1929. Meanwhile, almost all the "enlightened" German Jews of the 19th century had found it virtually impossible to win acceptance by their gentile neighbors. At best, they were regarded as historical curiosities, exceptions who proved the rule of Jewish separateness. Not even Moses Mendelssohn, the greatest historical curiosity of them all, had been able to aspire to membership in the semi-neutral society of a Freemason's lodge, let alone any other. His successors, because they too were regarded as separate, also remained clearly identifiable objects of scorn and attack. Jewish commercial successes during the industrial revolution, a process which caused hardship to many uprooted German gentiles, further helped to perpetuate anti-Jewish feelings. The growth of the yellow press helped to popularize them.

But in this Germany was not alone. Anti-Semitic charges also appeared with appalling regularity throughout Eastern Europe during the early 20th century. In France, the cradle of Emancipation, they had even been brought up to date with the accusation of treason hurled at the Jewish army officer, Alfred Dreyfus (1859-1935), during the 1890s. This exploitation of nationalism was an example which reactionary elements throughout Europe soon found it convenient to ape. The era of tolerance, with its

The blood libel revived in the "ritual murder" number of Julius Streicher's newspaper, *Der Stuermer*, May 1, 1934. The slogan at the foot of the page reads, "The Jews are our misfortune."

Ein grawsamlich geschicht Geschehen zu passaw Von den Juden als hernach volgt

Hye stilt Cristoff acht partickel des sa
crament auß der kirché. legt das in sein
taiché. hat sy darinné drei tag behalté

Hye schuet er die sacrament den juden
auff den tisch die vmuermaylrgt gewe
sen sein. darumb sy im ein gulde gaben.

Hye tragen die jude vñ schulklopffer.
die sacrament yn ir synagog. vnd vber
antwurtten dye den Juden.

Hye sticht pfeyl Jud das sacrament
auff irem altar. ist plut darauß gangen
das er vñ ander juden gesehen haben.

Hye teyllen sy auß dye sacramét schick
ten zwen partickel gen Prag. zwē gen
salzpurg. zwen yn die Newenstat

Hye verprenten sy die sacramét versu
chen ob vnser glaub gerecht wer floge
auß dem offen zwen engel vñ ij taube

Hye vecht man all Juden zu passaw
die dy sacramét gekaufft verschickt ge
stolen vnd verprant haben.

Hye furt mā sy fur gericht. verurtaylt
die vier getaufft. fackel mand kolman
vnd walich. sein gekopft worden.

Hye zereyst man den pfeyl vnd vettel
die das sacramét behylté. dz darnach
gestochen vnd verprant haben.

Hye verprent man sy mit sampt dē ju
den. die yn irem glauben blyben. vnd
vmb das sacrament gewyst haben.

Hye wirt der Cristoff des sacraments
verkauffer. auff einem wage zeryssen
mit gluenden zangen.

Hye hebt man an zw pawen. vnserm
herren zu lob eyn gotzhauß. Auß der
juden synagog zc.

Nach christi gepurt. M.CCCC.LXX
vñ.iar Regirende zu der zeyte, der hochwirdig furst vñ herr Vber
Vlrich zu passaw geborn vonn Nußdorff. Es hat sych begeben
das ein eychtfertiger vñ versager mensch weyland genant Cristoff eysen
greißhamer / vergessende seiner sel selygkayt / nach Judas syten auß beger
zeytlichs guts Abit den juden dye zeyt wonēde hye zu passaw / bey der Iltz
alda hinder sant Jorgen perg/ seynd vñ lesterer des gecreutzigten waren
lebentigen gots vñ Marie seiner geperyn yn ein vorret vertrag gemacht
hat. Nach dem als sy yn etwo offt in yren potschaffté genutzt vñ gebraucht
nahendt vnnd verr geschickt hetten. ob er yn precht das hochwirig sacra
ment. den leychnam vnsers herren Jhesu christi ob sy den icht kauffen wol
ten. darzu sy ym als die begyrigen hunnd. auß grossem neyd so sy zu dem her
ren Jesu vnserm heyland haben. antwort gaben. Er solt den pfenig darum
wolten sy ym ein benugen thun. nach solchem geding der verkauffer vnnd
verstockt sunder yn seiner poßhayt nach dem hochwirdigen sacrament stel
let. des bemelten sybenvndsybenzigsten iars. Am freytag vor sant Michia
els tag die kirchen vnser lieben frawen yn der freyung der abtey. das stock
geheuß auff gebrochen. daryn viij. partickel des hochwirdygen sacraments
gestollen. das mit seinen sundigen henden an gegryffen. vnd yn ein tuchlein
gewickelt von dem freytag byß an den suntag Morgen bey ym getragen dar
nach die Juden falschafftig vberantwurdt. vmb eyn reynischen guldē ver
kaufft. eyn partyckel gepurt vmb dreyssig pfennig. zu schmach der heyligen
christenlich kyrchen. dye Juden vnd lesterer gots das behalten. zu zweyfel
in ir synagog pracht den leychnam christi mit iren sundige benden. gryffen

mit grymiger gier zu creutzige. christē glaubē zu bewerē Ein jud ein schar
pfes messer genūme den leychnā xpi auff irem altar in die synagog gestochē
darauß plut gestossen. Eins kindes angesicht erschyne. Die jude lere erschra
cken. wurde iij. radt. vñ schickté.ij. partickel gen Prag. ij. in die Newstat.ij.
gen Saltzpurg.ij. partickel wolffen sy yn eine gluende packoffen. haben sy
gesehen.ij. engel.ij. tauben auß dem offen flyge. nachmals ist der vbelteyter
vor der fasten im sybenundzbentzg gst iare. bey eine kyrchstock zu Germal
perg begryffen vñ den gefange gefurt auß oberhaub bey passaw. Da
selbst er vngezwungē solch groß vbel gesagt vñ mer auff die Judicheyt. dar
auff der obgenant hochwirdig vñ got vater. vñ herr Vlrich byschoff zu pas
saw. Als ein christēlicher furst dem solch vbel pillich zu hertzen ist gangen.
vñ rechtlich zu straffen erkant h at. schuff durch bedenckeln vñ gestrenge Rit
ter herrē Sebastian vō der alben. die zeit seiner gnade marschalck. die selbe
Juden hye zu passaw all zu fahen vnd vmb die warhayt zu frage. die doch
also gemeynicklich einbellig vñ bekantlich wurde. vñ zaygte das messer. dē
stein. die stat vñ den ofen da sy solch hanblüg mit dem hoch wirdigen sacra
ment volbracht vñ begangē habē. Also bekerte sych yr vier zu dem Christē
lichen glaubē. vñ wurdē am Erichtag nach Judica yn der fasten des sybē
vndsybenzigstē iars fur recht gestellt. Die newē christē mit dem schwert ge
richt. die alt Jude yn dem fewer. auch ir zwen mit zange gerissen. Nach de als
vber etlich woche ward der verkauffer auch nach ordnūg des rechtē mit
gluende zangē gericht. das er als mit grosser gedult rew vñ andacht erlyde
hat wie das durch yn gehandelt ist. offentlich vor menigklich bekannt. got
wol sych vber sein vñ alle glaubig sel erbarmen. Amen.

A Nazi cartoon. The caption reads: "Otto Mayer, the Nuremberg Jew, used to crucify his victim. He bound her stark naked to a specially prepared wooden cross, and raped her as soon as the blood began to flow from her wounds."

Der Nürnberger Jude Otto Mayer

pflegte seine Opfer zu kreuzigen. In völlig nacktem Zustande band
er sie an ein eigens dazu angefertigtes Holzkreuz und schändete
sie, sobald aus den Wundmalen das Blut floß.

verbal respect for all creeds, had deprived them of a denominational excuse for their prejudicial hatreds. Instead, these elements cloaked their feelings in the garb of the interests of the state, whose guardians they claimed to be. It was not only in Germany, therefore, that the Jews were accused of forming an international coterie of intrigue, and not only there that the *Protocols of the*

German broadsheet, c. 1480, telling the story of the alleged desecration of the Host in Passau, Bavaria, 1478. 1) Christoff Eisengreisshamer, a Christian, steals eight consecrated wafers from St. Mary's Church. 2) He sells them, for one gulden, to the Jews, who are identified by their circular badge. 3) The Jews take the Host to the synagogue. 4) In reenactment of the crucifixion they stab the wafers, out of which blood flows. 5) They send some of the wafers to Prague and Salzburg. 6) When they try to burn the remaining wafers, in which the face of a child appears, two angels and two doves fly out of the oven. 7) The Passau Jews are arrested. 8) Two are beheaded. 9) Others are tortured and then burnt. 10) All the Jews who knew of the desecration are burned to death. 11) Christoff is torn to pieces with glowing pincers. 12) The synagogue is converted into a church (opposite).

101

Das größte Getreide-Wucherthier der Welt.

Neueste zoologische Entdeckung des Kikeriki.

Learned Elders of Zion were read with uncritical avidity.

More weight, therefore, should perhaps be given to two particularly German phenomena of the 19th century, conservatism and racialism. Both notions formed part of the backwash to the romantic and nationalist reaction to Napoleon's victories; both expressed an attempt to recapture the true nature of the pure German spirit, which had once ensured German greatness; both were apparently justified by Bismarck's extraordinary success in building the German Empire after 1870; and both were crystallized during the *Kulturkampf* which he waged against the dual loyalty of adherents to the Catholic Church.

Conservatism, the first element, implied absolute obedience to the ideal of the German nation-state. The argument that this institution took precedence over the individual had been inherent in much German philosophy ever since the turn of the 19th century. After 1870 it was expressed, even more eloquently, by Nietzsche, who claimed that the state recognized no morality either. Racialism, the second element, took a turn equally adverse to liberalism. Under the influence of its earliest proponents, the terms "Semitic" and "Aryan" lost their original references to two linguistic groups. As early as 1855 when Count Gobineau published his *Essay on the Inequality of the Human Races,* they had been transferred to the plain of human characteristics. In the hands of such later 19th century writers as Richard Wagner (1813-1883) the composer turned philosopher, and Houston Stewart Chamberlain (1855-1927) the Englishman turned German, the terms became descriptions of two distinct human species. The Jews (Semites) and the Germans (Aryans of pure Tuetonic stock) were said to be racially distinct; of the two, the Jews were said to be inferior in every way — physically, intellectually, and racially.

Despite their "scientific" pretensions, these were not arguments which the Jews could hope to counter rationally. Ultimately, their voluble attempts to do so served merely to

The Viennese anti-Semitic picture paper, *Kikeriki,* depicts the Jews as a world-devouring vampire.

enhance the prominence of the question in the public eye. Under no circumstances could the Jews claim, or be granted, inclusion in the national character, which had supposedly been fashioned in the Tuetonic forests and forged in the tribal past.

For it was on this basis that, in the late 19th century, traditional patterns of prejudice became modern ideologies of hate. In 1879 the term anti-Semitism was coined by William Marr (1818-1904), himself a renegade Jew. One year earlier Adolf Stoecker (1835-1909), Protestant chaplain at the Imperial court and the son of a jail warden, had formed the Christian Socialist Workers' Party. Although this body was neither Christian, nor Socialist, nor a union of workingmen, and although its activities were eventually supressed by the Emperor himself, it nevertheless occupies an important place in German history. It was the first political party to base its program on a specifically anti-Jewish plank. For that reason it was joined by members of the bourgeoisie and the aristocracy, and supported by a group of intellectuals who buttressed its propaganda with a veneer of pseudo-scientific nonsense.

Adolf Hitler needed to add nothing new to the ideology thus provided. Any refinements which might have been necessary were provided by history itself. Defeat in the first world war, a traumatic experience for the German people, was an overture to tragedy for the Jews. National humiliation, economic disintegration, and political extremism followed each other in swift succession. As a result of the cataclysm, Jewish casualties in defense of the Fatherland, Jewish losses during the inflation of the 1920s, and Jewish opposition to Bolshevism in the 1930s were all ignored. The fact that the "Hymn of Hate," the most popular German patriotic song of the war, had been composed by a Jew, Ernst Lissauer (1882-1937), was quietly forgotten. Instead, attention focused on Jewish support for the Weimar Republic politicians, the rise of Jewish business, and the "international" complexion of Jewish finance. Anti-Semitism, the most persistent

Facing pages from the *Bird's Head Haggadah,* from southern Germany, c. 1300. The page illustrates the hymn *Dayyeinu*. On the left, Moses is receiving the two Tablets of the Law while passing on five (an allusion to the five books of the Pentateuch). The human figures have birds' heads, so as not to transgress the biblical law prohibiting graven images.

Jewish badges decreed by the Nazis during their occupation of Europe in World War II. 1. Bulgaria, Poland (part), Lithuania, Hungary, Greece (part) 2. Germany, Alsace, Bohemia - Moravia 3. France 4. Holland 5. Greece, Serbia, Belgrade, Sofia 6. Belgium 7. Slovakia 8. Bulgaria 9. Slovakia 10.Poland (part), East and Upper Silesia.

theme in Hitler's ragbag of ideology, thus became the most attractive element in the National Socialist Party which he led.

Nazism

Hitler's determination to free Germany of the Jews by making life difficult for them was immediately apparent. In April 1933,

Identity card issued in Cologne, March, 1939, bearing the distinctive "J".

shops owned by Jews were boycotted and, in May, books written by them were burned. Throughout that year, the Jews were already subjected to the medieval indignity of the yellow badge and to the brutality of the Brownshirts. By 1935 the more subtle, but no less harsh, arm of legislation was called in to support the program of violence. The Nuremberg Laws of September 15, 1935, excluded the Jews from citizenship, public office, the professions, and the intellectual and artistic life of the

Nuremburg Laws

105

"For Aryans only." A bench in a Berlin park, 1938 (above). Nazi pickets outside a Jewish shop in Germany. The placard reads, "Germans! Defend yourselves! Don't buy from Jews " (below).

country. They also conjured up a new genealogical breed, the half-Jews and the quarter-Jews, of whom only the latter could be accepted as Germans. The Olympic Games of 1936, and the Nazis' consequent need to put on a show of humanity for the benefit of the rest of mankind, did provide a short respite. But they were soon followed by economic measures designed to "aryanize" Jewish business concerns; a racial census designed to emphasize Jewish ostracism; and the forcible imposition of the extra names "Sarah" or "Israel" to the identity papers of every Jewish woman and man. By 1939 only 15.6% of all German Jews had regular employment; and thousands were already in concentration camps.

In October 1938 a particularly refined form of barbarity took place. 15-17,000 German Jews of Polish origin were packed into trains, dumped on the Polish border, and there left to fend for themselves whilst the Polish government (itself notoriously anti-Semitic) decided their fate. Amongst the unfortunate crowd was one couple who felt constrained to send a tearful postcard to their 17 year old son, Herschel Grynszpan, an exile from Germany who was living in Paris. The boy had to do something; and did. On November 9, he shot the Third Secretary of the German embassy in Paris.

The Nazi reaction was immediate and violent. Whatever the extent of earlier anti-Jewish excesses, those of the night of the 9th of November outdid them all. On that *Kristallnacht* the Nazis conducted a nationwide pogrom; they smashed Jewish houses, burned Jewish synagogues, and beat and incarcerated Jewish men. In a final touch of German thoroughness, the Jewish community was also fined one billion Reichsmark to cover the cost of the damage. Violence had now become official state policy. *Kristallnacht*

Those German Jews who had initially tried to talk sense into the Nazis soon gave up the attempt. The majority gradually appreciated that their fate depended on their own efforts and could not be entrusted to the benevolence of the government.

Their only hope was emigration; their only source of strength was communal cohesion.

The Badge

The first result of this feeling was that German Jewry closed its ranks. For the first time in its history, the community began to act as a single body, first under the Central Committee for Aid and Construction and then within the newly created Reich Representation of the Jews in Germany. Their second reaction was to intensify Jewish public and cultural life. Jewish schools were established to accommodate those children excluded from public education, and the Jewish press was enlarged to provide some compensation for the lurid madness of the Nazi organ, *Der Stuermer*. The *Juedischer Rundschau* earned undying fame with its famous headline: "Wear it in pride — the yellow badge," and German Jews found new self-respect when they did just that. More joined Zionist parties than ever before, read books on Jewish subjects, and patronized the newly founded Jewish Cultural League. Indeed, between 1933 and 1938 the latter became "the largest voluntary union of Jews in Germany," and supported a mass of theater ensembles and musical societies.

Migration

The majority of the German community of half a million persons attempted to emigrate. The trend in this direction which had been merely a trickle before 1935 (when the process was relatively easy), became a flood thereafter (when it became very

Hershel Grynszpan in 1938. He was convicted for the assassination of a German diplomat in Paris but his fate is not known.

108

Als die Kreis-Synagogen-Gemeinde Insterburg ihre Vorbereitungen für den 22. Mai 1938 traf und diesen Tag des Gedenkens an Einhundert Jahre Bestehens mit zahlreichen Ehrengästen aus den Provinzgemeinden im Gotteshause festlich beging, ahnte sie es nicht, dass das Jahr 1938 des einhundertjährigen Bestehens gleichzeitig das Jahr ihres Unterganges bedeuten werde.

Am 10. November 1938, sechs Monate nach der Jubelfeier war es, in der Frühe zwischen 3 und 4 Uhr, als das schöne Gotteshaus, die Stätte einhundertjährigen jüdischen Lebens und Webens in der Stadt Insterburg, in Flammen aufging und es mit allem, was sie an Gedenktafeln und an sonstigen Denkwürdigkeiten aus der Zeit von 1838 bis 1938 enthielt, mit etwa 20 Thorarollen und ihren kostbaren Mänteln, mit wertvollen Vorhängen der heiligen Lade, mit der schönen Chuppa, mit einem klangvollen Harmonium, mit zwei Pianinos, mit zahlreichen Tallitim und Gebetbüchern von Gemeindemitgliedern, mit dem Ornat des Rabbiners, mit einer reichhaltigen Bibliothek u. a. in Schutt und Asche legte. - - - - - -

Einhundert Jahre jüdischen Lebens sind damit ausgelöscht, die Arbeit zielbewusster, kraftvoller führender Männer, die ihr Alles hingaben, der Gemeinde und dem Judentum zu dienen, sie ist umsonst gewesen; - eine Gemeinde, ausgestattet mit korporativen Rechten, mit einem Vorstande und einer Repräsentanten-Versammlung, die für eine ordnungsmässige Führung und Verwaltung sorgte, mit einem Rabbiner und einem Kantor, die jüdisches Leben und Wissen garantierten, - sie ist nicht mehr. - - - Ein von einem Bretterzaun umgebener, an zwei Strassenfronten gelegener freier Platz deutet z. Z. noch die Stelle an, auf welcher unsere erhabene Synagoge gestanden hat.

Nur ein winzig kleiner Rest von Mitgliedern unter Führung des Seniors der Gemeinde, des allverehrten zeitigen Vorstehers Herrn J o s e f K a d o r im biblischen Alter von 81 Jahren, bildet den Bestand einstiger Grösse der Gemeinde. Diesem Restbestande gelingt es einstweilen noch, an Sabbaten und Festtagen Gottesdienst abzuhalten, den der langjähr. frühere Schriftführer der Repräs.-Versammlung, Herr David Simon, in einem Betraume mit Sachkenntnis leitet.

Wie lange dieses zusammengeschrumpfte Häuflein noch eine jüdische Einheit bilden wird,

das liegt in Deiner Hand, Du grosser, erhabener Gott;

Erbarme Dich unser, erbarme Dich des ganzen jüd. Volkes!

Insterburg, 24. April 1941.

Josef Israel Wieszenke

"Farewell message." Last entry in the Insterburg (East Prussia) community book, begun in 1860. It was written to the members by the head of the community on the eve of their deportation by the Nazis and is dated April 24, 1941.

The Ohel Yakob Synagogue of Munich on the morning after *Kristallnacht,* 1938.

difficult). Despite the quotas imposed by the prospective countries of reception, and despite the heavy fines imposed by the German government, over 300,000 Jews had left the country by 1939. Of these, 63,000 went to the United States and 40,000 to Great Britain. Another 55,000 had gone to Palestine. There they had been channeled by the Zionist Palestine Office which organized training farms, Hebrew schools, and even (in a unique display of Nazi-Zionist co-operation) the transfer of Jewish capital through the *Ha'avarah* company.

The outbreak of the second world war merely intensified the various processes already under way. Those Jews who could do so continued to leave Germany, and about 70,000 more escaped before October 1941. Those who could not, experienced further terror. Under the terms of the Final Solution they were all

Judenrein

110

gradually deported to Theresienstadt or Auschwitz, and on May 19, 1943, Germany was officially declared "free of Jews" (*Judenrein*).

Even in this hour the community had been provided with a *Leo Baeck* remarkable leader, in the person of Rabbi Leo Baeck (1873-1956). Born in Poland and educated at the Berlin Hochschule,

Leo Baeck, rabbi and theologian. He refused to take advantage of an opportunity to flee Germany, preferring to remain and share the fate of his community.

Baeck's academic achievements, eloquent sermons, and innumerable acts of kindness had won him honor long before Hitler had come to power. Later, as head of the Reich Representation Council, he also won respect. He spurned a Nazi invitation to emigrate in 1938, vowing that he would only leave when there was no longer a quorum of ten Jews (a *minyan*) left in the country. After 1943 he was equally stubborn in his refusal to succumb to the brutality of Theresienstadt. Instead, by his bearing, behavior, and leadership there he became a living incarnation of the affirmative faith he preached. He infused thousands of his

111

fellow sufferers with the unshakeable belief that survival was a
moral obligation, even in the depths of the Nazi hell. Baeck did
not return to Germany after the war. Instead, he accepted the
professorship of theology at Cincinnati. Not every Jew followed
his example. Between 1945 and 1960 about 6,000 German Jews
returned to Germany, and some 2,000 Jews from other countries
settled there. This was in addition to the number of former

Dedication ceremony of the new Jewish community center in Berlin, 1959.

Deported Persons (about 6,000 in 1960) who had remained to
form a significant portion of the congregations in Munich and
Frankfort.

Initially, the decision taken by these Jews to settle in Germany aroused intense controversy. The Zionist movement was
especially opposed to it, and questioned the morality of any
permanent Jewish residence in what had become known as "the
accursed land." Against the Zionist viewpoint were ranged those
who called for the building of new bridges between the Jewish
and the German peoples. Ultimately the latter voices proved, if

112

not the loudest, then certainly the more persuasive. Konrad Adenauer's sustained efforts to ensure world recognition for the moral rehabilitation of his country removed the fear of persistent anti-Semitism. The Government of Israel's agreement to accept reparations in September 1952 removed the stigma of ostracism. Finally, West Germany's "economic miracle" during the 1950s and 1960s added the inducement of financial advantage.

Former West German Chancellor Konrad Adenauer with Dr. Nahum Goldmann, on his visit to Jerusalem, 1966.

Nevertheless, post-war German Jewry has become an abnormal community. Its position is to some extent symbolized by the change in its nomenclature, from *Deutsche Juden* ("German Jews") to *Juden in Deutschland* ("Jews in Germany"). In both numbers (about 26,000) and influence the community is but a shadow of its former greatness. Even its very chances of survival cannot be put very high. The various congregations lack sufficient teachers, community workers, and rabbis. Its death rate exceeds its birth rate, and, despite the shadow cast by history, the rate of intermarriage between Jews and Germans is amongst the highest in the world.

"Jews in Germany"

113

Signing the German-Israel reparations agreement, 1952.
Moshe Sharett, at the time foreign minister of Israel
and later prime minister, is signing, while to his right
is Dr. Nahum Goldmann, one of the main architects
of the agreement.

Only in the sphere of relations between the two sovereign *The State of* states of West Germany and Israel can relations be said to be *Israel* approaching normality. The first step in this direction was taken on September 10, 1952, when the reparations agreement was signed by the representatives of the two governments. From this flowed a large number of commercial and diplomatic contacts (although not cultural) which extended far beyond the limits originally envisaged. The second step was taken on May 12, 1965, when diplomatic relations between the two countries were formally established. It was followed, in July 1965, by an exchange of ambassadors. Despite some initial opposition within Israel, and despite occasional outbreaks of anti-Semitism in Germany, Israeli-German relationships have become increasingly cordial thereafter. Adenauer in May 1966 and Ehrhard in November 1967 were both former West German chancellors who visited Israel.

114

Prime Minister Golda Meir greeting Chancellor Willie Brandt of West Germany on the latter's arrival at Lydda airport, June, 1973.

The third, and possibly final, step towards normality was taken in June 1973. Willy Brandt then became the first chancellor in office to undertake a journey to the Jewish state. His first official engagement was a visit to Yad Vashem, the national memorial to the victims of Nazism. It was in that sombre, stark, and harshly simple building that he read a passage from the Book of Psalms:

> The Lord is righteous in His acts;
> He brings justice to all who have been wronged.
> He taught Moses to know His way
> and showed the Israelites what He could do.
> The Lord is compassionate and gracious,
> long suffering and for ever constant;
> He will not always be the accuser
> or nurse His anger for all times.

SOURCES

page

2   In the words of one historian . . . – A.J.P. Taylor, *The Course of German History,* (1946), p. 1.

4   "in order to enhance . . ." – J. Aronius, *Regesten zur Geschichte der Juden . . .,* (1902), 70 no. 168.

5   occasional Jewish reprisals . . . – A.M. Habermann (ed.), *Sefer Gezerot Ashkenaz ve-Ẓarefat,* (1945), pp. 30-31a, 33, 34, 97, 99-100.

6   At Mainz Jews threw their money . . . – H.H. Ben-Sasson, *Perakim be-Toledot Yisrael bi-Mei ha-Beinayim,* (1962).

7   No wonder that by that year . . . – H.H. Ben-Sasson, *Toledot Am-Yisrael bi-Mei ha-Beinayim,* (1969).

11   Instead, because Protestantism . . . – see the letter written in 1525 by Abraham ben Eliezer ha-Levi in *Kirjath Sepher,* 7 (1930/31), p. 444-5.

13   The daughters went even further . . . – J. Katz, *Out of the Ghetto,* (1973), p. 84 and 236 n. 11.

17   The Jews, he objected . . . – F. Eyck, *The Frankfurt Parliament,* (1968), pp. 241-3.

19   As he put it . . . – quoted in H.M. Sachar, *The Course of Modern Jewish History,* (1958), p. 143.

22   to some part of the Middle East – Genesis 10:3; Jeremiah 51:27.

23   The rabbis therefore lengthened . . . – J.D. Eisenstein, *Oẓar Dinim u-Minhagim,* (1917), p. 46 ff.

25   No wonder . . . – Responsa "Rosh" 20:20.

25   Fear of derision . . . – Isserles to *Shulḥan Arukh, Oraḥ Hayyim* 554-17.

25   The specter of destitution . . . – Isserles to *Shulḥan Arukh, Yoreh De'ah* 133 and Tosafot to *Avodah Zara* 57b.

27   The irregularity of sustenance . . . – J. Meminster, *Leket Yosher,* (1923), vol. 1 p. 74.

27   And the danger of mob attack . . . – A.I. Sperling, *Ta'amei Ha-Minhagim,* (1896), vol. 2, nos. 19f., p. 4a quoting *Likkutei ha-Pardes.*

27   Young men . . . – Tosafot to Sukkot 45a.

27   Jacob ben Moses Moellin . . . – *Maharil* (1558), 38b, 41b.

27   Before 1096, especially . . . – I. Agus, *The Heroic Age of Franco-German Jewry,* (1969), pp. 341-2.

page

28   The popular *Ḥad Gadya*... – D. Goldschmidt, *Haggadah Shel Pesaḥ, Mekoroteha ve-Toledoteha,* (1960), pp. 96-98.

32   It was, rather, the Yiddish vowel system ... – H. Yalon, *"Le-Toledot Hagiyat ha-Ivrit be-Ashkenaz"* in *Inyenei Lashon,* (1942/43), p. 52-58.

34   The tosafist tradition originated ... – E.E. Urbach, *Ba'alei ha-Tosafot,* (1955).

35   "never conceded a point" – according to Rabbenu Tam in *Sefer ha-Yashar* (1959), no. 64.

40   After also outlining ... – *Etwas ueber die Rabbinische Literatur,* (1819).

42   In general, medieval German Jews ... – G. Scholem, *Major Trends in Jewish Mysticism,* (1955), p. 80.

44   Thus it teaches ... – *Sefer Ḥasidim* (ed. Jerusalem, 1966), para. 415, 116.

44   It warns the tax-payer ... – H.H. Ben-Sasson, *Perakim be-Toledot Yisrael bi-Mei ha-Beinayim* (1962), pp. 189-190.

47   Jacob Emden and Jonathan Eybeschuetz ... – A. Shohet, *Ha-Mashber ha-Ruḥani ve-ha-Dati...,* (1960).

50   But Mendelssohn's German disciples ... – M. Pelli, "Intimations of Religious Reform in the German Hebrew Haskalah Literature," in *Journal of Jewish Studies,* 32 (1970), pp. 3-13.

54   The latter not only preached ... – *Ueber die Autonomie der Rabbinen und das Prinzip der Juedischen Ehe,* (1843).

54   The only changes ... – L. Ginzberg, *Students, Scholars, Saints,* (1928), pp. 195-216.

56   He preached that the Jews ... – S.R. Hirsch, *Nineteen Letters,* no. 17.

57   "a rabble of unclean birds",– E. Landau, *Zelaḥ* to *Berakhot,* (Prague, 1791), introduction.

62   As he wrote to a Christian colleague ... – M. Buber, *Theologische Blaetter,* 12 (1933), p. 273.

63   The German Emperor Barbarossa ... – S. Baron, *A Social and Religious History of the Jews,* (1952), vol. 4, p. 80.

66   A close reading of Deuteronomy ... – Deuteronomy 23:20.

67   As the tosafists pointed out ... – Tosafot to *Bava Meẓia* 70b.

67   About a century after ... – C. Roth, "The Jew in the Middle Ages" in *The Cambridge Medieval History,* 7(1932), p. 645.

68   "the most permanent ..." – S. Baron, *The Jewish Community, its History and Structure to the American Revolution,* (1942), vol. 2, p. 100.

70   "In this way the banker ..." – S. Stern, *The Court Jew,* (1950), p. 9.

73   Notwithstanding an inadequate trial . . . – S. Eidelberg, "A Note on Joseph Süss Oppenheimer's death sentence," in *Journal of Jewish Studies,* 30(1968), pp. 272-4.

78   As early as April 10, 1933, an English newspaper . . . – *The Daily Telegraph.*

80   The inferior status of an "imperial servant" – *Servi Camerae Regis;* see S. Baron, *A Social and Religious History of the Jews,* (1965), vol. 9, pp. 135-192, 308-331.

83   Since the Christian Authorities . . . – G. Kisch, *The Jew in Medieval Germany,* (1970), p. 306.

83   As early as the 11th century, community ordinances . . . – Responsa Maharam of Rothenburg (ed. Prague, 1895) nos. 918 and 932.

84   as in 14th century Worms . . . – S. Baron, *The Jewish Community, its History and Structure to the American Revolution,* (1942), vol. 2, p. 47.

85   He was widely referred to as Me'or ha-Golah . . . – a phrase apparently first used by Rashi. J. Mueller (ed.), *Teshuvot Ḥakhmei Ẓarefat ve-Lofer,* (1881), no. 21.

85   Amongst the many famous *takkanot* . . . – see Responsa Meir of Rothenburg (ed. Prague, 1895), nos. 886 and 1121.

88   They dealt with such diverse matters . . . – L. Finkelstein, *Jewish Self-Government in the Middle Ages,* (1924), pp. 218-251.

88   When in 1603 a large gathering of rabbis . . . – H.H. Ben-Sasson, *Toledot Am Yisrael bi-Mei ha-Beinayim,* (1969), pp. 286-8.

96   hence the sobriquet *protestrabbiner* . . . – a phrase coined by Herzl in *Die Welt,* vol. 1, no. 7 (July 16, 1897).

99   Not even Moses Mendelssohn . . . – J. Katz, *Jews and Freemasons in Europe, 1729-1939,* (1970).

103   Conservatism, the first element . . . – J. L. Talmon, "Mission and Testimony," in *The Unique and the Universal,* (1965), pp. 119-164.

103   Ultimately, their voluble attempts . . . – I. Schorsch, *Jewish Reactions to German Anti-Semitism, 1870-1914,* (1972).

108   Indeed, between 1933 and 1938, the latter became . . . – H. Freeden, *Juedisches Theater in Nazideutschland,* (1964), p. 1.

Encyclopaedia Judaica, Jerusalem, 1972, under: Ashkenazim, Germany, Ḥasidei Ashkenaz, and individual people and places.

Arendt, Hannah, *The Origins of Totalitarianism,* New York, 1966.
Finkelstein, Louis, *Jewish Self-Government in the Middle Ages,* New York, 1964.
Holborn, Hajo, *A History of Modern Germany,* New York, 1959 - 69.
Katcher, Leo, *Post-Mortem,* New York, 1968.
Kisch, Guido, *The Jews in Medieval Germany,* New York, 1970.
Liptzin, Solomon, *Germany's Stepchildren,* Cleveland, 1961.
Lowenthal, Marvin, *The Jews of Germany,* Philadelphia, 1936.
Marcus, Jacob Rader, *The Jew in the Medieval World,* New York, 1969.
Reitlinger, Gerald, *The Final Solution,* London, 1968.
Stern, Selma, *The Court Jew,* Philadelphia, 1950.
Zimmels, Hirsch Jakob, *Ashkenazim and Sephardim,* London, 1958.